Growing with
the Organic Movement:

Perspectives from WWOOF Farms in the USA

Camille B. Glenn

DEDICATION

For my husband Dave, farmer and author

iv

ACKNOWLEDGEMENTS

To all of the WWOOF hosts that kindly and generously contributed their stories, "mahalo"; without these I could not have written this book.

Table of Contents

"Teaching kids how to feed themselves and how to live in a community responsibly is the center of an education."

Alice Waters

Preface

This book describes various shared experiences of a number of WWOOF farm hosts across America with the intention of informing the reader about what it involves to share your organic farming experience with volunteers who are desirous of learning about sustainable living and what it takes to grow food organically.

I am sincerely grateful to each of the Wwoof hosts who somehow found the time in their very busy farm lives to share their thoughts with me. I have learned much from them, and without their input this book literally could not have been written. Some of the hosts were too busy "down on the farm" to write very much, or at all, which is so very understandable, but I appreciate their attempts nevertheless; all of the contributions, short or long, have been invaluable in enabling me to compile the experiences of being Wwoof hosts and my attempt to express our collective ideas. For example, Margo from Maravilla Mountain in Puerto Rico said she didn't have time to really contribute because she was so busy at this time, but at the same time she did share how she recognized the value of the Wwoofers on her farm. She wrote, "Although I have to add, if I didn't have volunteers, I wouldn't be able to write these few sentences. It's been mostly good, and we have had some return for a few seasons."

Some have chosen to remain anonymous which I fully respect, so their comments have been incorporated into the information you read. Some hosts were not only willing, but eager to share their opinions which was very helpful, and many of these found the time to share quite a bit more information, and I am very grateful to have included their stories, or fragments of their stories. A recurring thought expressed by the current hosts has been how they are looking forward to continuing to host many more wonderful Wwoofers on their farms over the next years, and my husband and I agree.

Wishing all farm hosts, from the ones just starting out to the ones far more experienced than us, the best of WWoofing experiences as we all participate in the growing organic movement. And to all future farmers and Wwoofers I will share the words of the poet Gary Snyder when he said something many years ago, around the time when I was first exploring rural life,

"Find your place on the planet and dig in."

"A healthy social life is found only when in the mirror of each soul the whole community finds its reflection."

Rudolf Steiner

Chapter One

An Introduction to
Wwoofing, Sustainable Living
& the Organic Movement

Organic farming, sustainable living, and the world of Wwoofing (Note for the newcomers: WWOOF is the acronym for *Worldwide Opportunities on Organic Farms)* are converging aspects of the Organic Movement. This organic movement has been gaining momentum for nearly half a century and its roots can be traced back even further to the early part of the twentieth century, and in some opinions to the very beginning of the industrial revolution. In the first dozen years of this century the number of organic farms has been increasing substantially, even while the numbers remain small in comparison to industrialized agriculture. And an increasingly large number of people, both young and young in heart, are joining this movement with enthusiasm, ideals, and an eagerness to grow through and with this movement and take it to new heights. In fact, if you ever wonder where your food comes from, if you choose organic and local foods when you shop and cook, if you care about the earth and her resources and about the future supply of our water, if you are interested in off-grid living, using solar energy or other alternative energy, or if you are just curious about any of these issues, then you are already a part of the organic movement no matter how directly or indirectly involved you are. Technically the organic movement specifically refers to organic farming, but the scope of WWOOF and the lifestyle of the organic farms mentioned throughout this book encompass all of the related ideas discussed above.

WWOOF organizations provide the means for people of all ages who wish to directly experience and learn about organic farming and sustainable living to connect directly with host farms that are willing and able to share their knowledge. As members of the organizations, hosts and Wwoofers contact one another to inquire and make arrangements for the exchanges. The clear purpose is for agricultural and cultural exchanges, presenting education in growing food organically and living with sustainable practices. This is all accomplished, without any exchange of money, and is taught informally yet directly at the source, providing ample opportunity for anyone who wants to learn about the true source of their food to reconnect with nature, and to try their hand at rewarding physical labor voluntarily with the express desire of learning. Since Wwoofers come from all over the world, the hosts' world is opened up to cultural exchanges that wouldn't be possible otherwise. Everyone learns and participates from shared living, with farms varying quite a bit in the nature of the living arrangements. In some situations helpers live in the home with the host families, in others they live in separate quarters, and in still others in their own tents on the land of the host farm. Food is provided in addition to accommodation arrangements, but while some hosts prepare meals, others encourage cooking together with the helpers, and still others provide food for Wwoofers to cook separately; or it may be a hybrid situation.

Wwoofing is often eye-opening for young people who have never left the city before and even if some have had gardening experience, they find rural living a welcome new challenge. Many focus on the idea of learning about the new culture they are exposed to, especially if they come from other countries, and likewise the hosts enrich their lives while living with and teaching the foreign participants. So we see that Wwoof itself is the connection that brings it all together.

The intention of this book is to continue looking into the unique culture of Wwoofing, primarily through the eyes and experiences of the Wwoof farm hosts across America, while also offering some information regarding the typical, or atypical Wwoofers, and to explore the relationship of WWOOF to the organic movement and sustainable living. There is a wealth of information available to us about organic farming through numerous books, magazines and of course the internet, and there are some wonderful books and blogs already available of first-hand accounts of Wwoofing, both across the USA and abroad, written by participants, and blogs by organic farmers, but the emphasis here is clearly on the hosts' perspectives on Wwoofing as it relates to their overall sustainable farm lifestyles. I will mention one book written by a Wwoofer which provides his very interesting and informative personal story of his adventures while Wwoofing. It is entitled *Farming Around the Country: An Organic Odyssey*, by Brian Bender.

As a WWoof host myself together with my husband Dave (who really runs the farm), I became interested in hearing from other hosts and in sharing their collective thoughts. I find the descriptions of the farms endlessly interesting. There are a tremendous amount of varied crops that are being raised and a vast array of different lifestyles and habitats within our organic communities. Many share similarities; for example, growing nutritious staple vegetables is a primary focus for quite a large number of farms, and then many of those are marketing through Farmers' Markets and CSAs (Community Supported Agriculture). However, there is also quite a large number of unusual farms, and I am including a few of these to show the diversity of possibilities as well as a mix of farms from different regions of the country. I was fortunate to be able to country. I was fortunate to be able to include responses from forty-seven states and Puerto Rico. There are interesting and informative forums on the WWOOF USA site that some hosts participate in and one can find a plethora of shared ideas and lively debates. There are forums that are only usable by Wwoofers, some only for hosts to participate in, and others that invite participation from both sides. I contacted some of those participants as springboards for further development of ideas presented here. However, it is also my intention that this book provides a somewhat different, and bit more extensive insight since it includes a broader spectrum of farms that I have been corresponding with in person, by phone, and through e-mail, and getting informative responses from them where they had not been writing on the forums. From what I have been told in many instances of correspondence, many farm hosts can benefit from these shared perspectives, particularly if they are still new to Wwoofing or if they are just considering becoming a host farm. For example, one host farm member expressed that as new hosts they have lots of worries and concerns and so are looking forward to reading what other hosts around the country who have had a few or more Wwoofers are experiencing. Hopefully prospective Wwoofers will also benefit from an inside look at farm hosts' experiences and expectations, although I presume this will be even more appealing to hosts, past, present and future. Current hosts of course can access all of the descriptions of farms on the WWOOF site, but I will highlight a few dozen of the more than 1500 farm listings within these pages to give a cross-section of the varied activities going on. I find the descriptions so interesting, and would truly love to take a trip cross-country and visit every one, perhaps Wwoofing my way across. My research has been so informative and leaves me in awe in many cases of just how much some farms accomplish. This is not intended to be a comprehensive survey of hosts, nor can it possibly hope to cover all the varied day-to- day events on a multitude of farms, nor all of the views. I didn't intentionally exclude anyone, but as I queried as many farms as possible and read through all the responses, I tried in particular to express ideas that will give the most insight into the role of the Wwoof host and the advice that I believe will be most valuable to pass on to others. As a host reading this you may find familiar situations, you might realize more that you are not alone in what you are experiencing through WWOOF, and occasionally you may find some surprising or opposing ideas that you can learn from.   If you are a farmer considering becoming a Wwoof host, you may become better informed and prepared to take the plunge. It may also bring up additional questions and send you to the forums to work out individual concerns. Anyone else reading just for curiosity might find themselves joining the WWOOF organization and exploring the organic movement first hand, learning how to live sustainably.

The concept of "organic farm" has become quite broad and more and more smaller family homesteads that grow their own food, and urban centers that are teaching life skills and/or perhaps providing food to within communities are also part of this growing organic movement. There are some farms that are primarily teaching centers that also take on Wwoofers at certain times and under different circumstances than regular interns or students. As more and more Americans (and of course this is global, so we see these same situations worldwide) seek new ways to eat healthy food and to have more control over their food sources, there are new seekers who want to try their hand at farming, even if only for a weekend at a time, as the original WWOOF organization founder started out doing. Others arrive at a WWOOF situation primarily because of environmental concerns and a desire to do no harm to the earth and become stewards of the land, soil, and water though conservation methods. So we see that all of these roads introduce newcomers into the growing organic movement.

For those relatively new or even unfamiliar with WWOOF here is a brief background. Wwoofing was started in England back in 1971 by a young woman, Sue Coppard, who was living and working as a secretary in the city of London. She sought to experience rural living in a meaningful way and to participate in growing organic food, and in learning how the food was being grown. She envisioned it as an exchange about agriculture and as a cultural or social exchange. She offered "helping hands" in exchange for the opportunity, and besides herself she started to bring other interested friends and colleagues. It started slowly, and through the help of published stories and word of mouth it grew, and kept growing, and they had such great experiences that it continued to grow by leaps and bounds and spread from the United Kingdom to continental Europe. It existed there for some time before coming "across the pond" to the USA, and internationally it still flourishes and grows within Europe, Asia, Africa, South America, Australia and the South Pacific, with new member countries continually joining. The founder is still very much involved with the original international WWOOF organization. *[This book just focuses on the farms in the United States, but references information regarding Wwoofers who come from all parts of the world.]*

Sustainable living is one of the underlying concepts that constitute Wwoofing. Unlike the world of consumerism, those who seek to live sustainably are getting in touch with the resources we use in our environment, primarily the soil for growing food, and the land for raising livestock, and the water we need for every aspect of our lives. The corresponding aim is to live in a way that respects those resources and ensures that they are not depleted, but rather that the circle of life is able to continue indefinitely. Along with these come issues of recycling, starting with natural animal fertilizers which are used to grow the plants rather than using chemicals, and very importantly composting and mulching, soil and water conservation, as well as recycling in the home, and using alternative sources of power from solar to wind to hydroelectric. Not all will be employed on each farm, but most components will be found. To live sustainably makes one think about how far so much of our food travels before reaching us as consumers, and brings up issues related to transportation and how this (negatively) impacts the environment. "Buying Local" is a huge factor in sustainable living; it supports the local farms and economy and reduces environmental concerns at the same time. "Farm-to–table" is another vital concept directly related, as farmers seek not only to grow the food organically, but also to create value-added products (for example, cheese, or jam, or coffee) for the consumer who benefits by knowing the complete source of their food. Taken one step further, more and more farms present a complete dining experience where meals are prepared and served from products entirely produced on their farms. These may be monthly or annual farm events, or be incorporated through a restaurant on or near the farm. Related to this is the grassroots Slow Food Movement, started in Italy in 1989, with more than 100,000 members worldwide today. They are strongly committed to both the community and the environment, supporting small-scale and sustainable production of food. Their philosophy promotes "good, clean, and fair food for all", recognizing "the strong connections between plate, planet, people, and culture." They have created the term "co-producer" to refer to those people who actively participate in the production of food rather than merely being consumers, so I see how participating in WWOOF directly correlates to these concepts. Sustainable Agriculture has become almost synonymous with organic farming or vice-versa, and as such they overlap. The ever increasing consumer demand for organic food products supports local small farmers through the Farmers' Markets and the CSAs and other direct purchase systems in place. Once again WOOF farms teaching Wwoofers, who in turn may farm their own lands one day, are all part of the chain of sustainable living. But as the movement grows in fact larger commercial farms are starting to emerge since the demand on the small farms is greater than the supply available. That is beyond the scope of this book, but it is easy to see that as the organic movement grows, large scale farming will naturally be involved and we hope that the very practices referred to here will translate effectively on the larger commercial farms. But the important thing is the growing trend across mainstream America (and again globally) to embrace organically grown food, and so the movement is inevitably growing, and Wwoofers and Wwoof hosts are active participants in this growth. The term organic farming is generalized to encompass methods of growing food without chemical fertilizers, without synthetic pesticides (herbicides, fungicides, and insecticides), without antibiotics or hormones, without food additives, and without GMOs. It is regulated internationally and nationally, but there are differences in the standards and practices to some degree within various regulating agencies. There is the Certified Organic designation, and there is Certified Naturally Grown which is an alternate farm assurance program for small-scale organic farmers. Most people are familiar with the National Organic Program and its USDA Certified Organic logo; the alternative program still follows all of the USDA standards, but requires less stringent record-keeping and inspection processes as it is tailored to accommodate the needs of small-scale mixed-agriculture farms. But they can't use the word "organic", so this becomes a very personal choice, and many farms still farm organically but do not complete either formal process of regulation. Sustainable agriculture produces food through maintaining healthy soil and the entire ecosystem. Farmers have to rely on biodiversity and learn what is best for their local conditions in order to follow the principles. While chemical farming used extensive inputs of all the items excluded in organic agriculture, the exact opposite applies. Hand labor becomes increasingly a large component of the farming process and Wwoofers definitely experience this as weeding replaces pesticides. Farming sustainably includes awareness and avoidance of excessive tillage which causes erosion and in preventing inadequate irrigation drainage which causes salinization. Farms must consider the relationship of the sun, water, air and soil on their farm sites. Over time and with much labor (again benefited greatly through additional help from Wwoofers) the soil quality gradually improves providing the right growing conditions. Sustainable agriculture also looks at economic profitability as well as economic equity in addition to the environmental stewardship of the land. An underlying principle is awareness now that what we do impacts future generations. It also considers social responsibility including the working and living conditions of the farm workers in addition to the stewardship of the land and natural resources. It is a tall order to satisfy our human food (and fiber) needs while making the best use of the natural resources, especially non-renewable ones, while sustaining the economics of farming. The socioeconomic aspects are not necessarily the focus of the WWOOF-Organic Farm model, but one example of this is that food grown and sold locally does not require additional energy for transportation. Contrary to all of the glowing ideas about organic farming and sustainable agriculture is the critical thought that since organic farming relies on many hands and is so labor intensive, and increasingly uses volunteer exchanges to keep going, then perhaps it is not truly sustainable. That is certainly food for thought as we develop our small-scale farms, and brings up questions for us to consider.

Organic farming is the main connection between the people who are stewarding the Wwoof farms and the Wwoofers who will be learning and helping on the farms. These farmers are growing food from every part of the food chain in a sustainable way. Each farm is using organic principles in cultivating the soil and raising their livestock, as much as possible, ideally completely, with many still in transition from chemical farming. Whether the farming element is just a small scale, non-commercial family homestead, or a mid-sized farm doing CSAs and Farmers' Markets, or even a large commercial farm, the teaching and learning still cover the principles of living and growing organically and sustainably. For the majority of Wwoofers, even if they already have ideals and ideas about eating organically and living a healthy lifestyle, this may be the first time they get to experience this life and to learn to understand both the challenges and the joys of growing food firsthand.

The information here shares the experiences of the WWOOF hosts and how the WWOOF program works for them, the unique situations they have had, and the common ones that have readily emerged. The specifics and variables of the many aspects and ways to accomplish individual goals of growing organically are beyond the scope of this book. But I'd like to present some basic information about key components of organic agriculture and persons who have been influential in the Organic Movement, and their related methods of growing food. Not everyone agrees on the precise beginning of organic farming, but it has its roots in the industrial revolution where chemical industrialized farming began. Nor was everyone amenable to the dramatic turnover, despite its promise of more food with less labor from less land. The negative side effects of the chemicals hadn't been factored in then, nor could anyone foresee just how much consumers would revolt against it. Perhaps it took the internet and expanding knowledge to spread the word, as we see today how more and more people are aware of the negative effects of chemically grown food and again are strongly demanding healthier, clean food.

In the early part of the twentieth century Rudolf Steiner taught principles of organic farming in Germany that he termed Biodynamic Agriculture, and in the 1940s Albert Howard developed organic agriculture techniques in England. By the 1950s in America J.I. Rodale continued with extensive research promoting organic growing along with healthy sustainable lifestyles, and the Rodale Press went on to publish substantial information including the magazine *Organic Farming and Gardening*. Steiner's principles of Biodynamics took hold with one of his students, Alan Chadwick, who was instrumental in teaching many in the USA, primarily in the 1970s, in conjunction with the back to the land movement. A student of his, John Jeavons, continues today teaching intensive gardening methods that are widely acclaimed, and his books are an excellent reliable, informative resource. From Asia Dr. Cho Han-kyu has created his method of sustainably growing nutritious food called Korean Natural Farming. His intent is to teach us how to grow food locally and economically in harmony with the natural environment. The system focuses on gathering indigenous micro-organisms which are present locally in the air and soil in order to beneficially grow plants and to create natural inputs for pest control with no need for chemicals. Korean Natural Farming is akin to Bokashi composting using effective microorganisms; this was developed in Okinawa, Japan by Teruo Higa. Natural Farming can also refer to the approach developed by Masanoba Fukuoka in Japan who designated his agricultural philosophy as "shizen noho", and which is also referred to as the Fukuoka method, or "do-nothing farming". This however does not refer to lack of labor, but rather to the avoidance of manufactured imputs. Mycorrihizae fungal inoculants are related to these concepts and are also popularly used by many farmers to improve and benefit plant growth through the symbiotic relationship between the fungi and the plants' roots. Permaculture develops sustainable and self-maintained agricultural systems modeled after natural ecosystems. Common practices include agroforestry, sheet mulching, and using rainwater harvesting. Bill Mollison is widely recognized for this method and lectures globally teaching permaculture design. Those give us a peek into some of the key methods employed by organic farmers using sustainable agriculture, and they are the ones most often mentioned by contributing hosts. Despite the differing methodologies that farmers choose, organic farmers are in agreement about being in control of our own food production, in growing healthy, nutritious food, and in employing sustainable ways to accomplish this.

The Wwoof farms present these opportunities to the Wwoofers, who can choose among all the variations and decide to volunteer where they can learn the practices best suited to their own philosophies or needs.

"It is one of the beautiful compensations in life that no man can sincerely help another without helping himself."

Ralph Waldo Emerson

Chapter Two

Exploring the Wwoof Farms

Wwoof hosts and Wwoofers are integrally related–we just can't have one without the other. Organic farms can exist independently of course, and future farmers or the merely curious can go on merrily without ever connecting with any of these farms. But the essence of Wwoofing is in bringing these two components together to create a unique world of agriculture and cultural exchange. WWOOF is the essential link. I will continue with the hosts and their farms because even a Wwoofer must begin with somewhere to go; after all, the farms must first be there for helpers come to!

There are astonishingly wonderful diverse farms to be found all across the country, in all fifty states, and even including farms in Puerto Rico and the U.S. Virgin Islands for helpers to come to. Farms within milder climates and within close access to large populated cities tend to have more farming openings and/or attract a larger number of applicants it seems. However, you will find numerous farms in other states that are equally full of opportunities to learn and still have year round activities whether or not they are actively growing because the climate is warm. Many use heated greenhouses year round, and if it is animal husbandry the weather is irrelevant, because naturally they need care on a daily basis. As hosts we can share these ideas with Wwoofers and help them spread their horizons.

Many of the traveling Wwoofers are also seeking adventures beyond farming and so naturally want to combine the two aspects. It is a great way to combine travel with learning and farming. They could often be Wwoofing in their own backyard so to speak, by looking for local farms, and many do this within commuting distance from their homes. This is a good way to tread lightly on our planet. But often the yearning to explore new places wins out, and as an avid traveler I understand this well. There is also some overlap with Helpxers, (Helpx is a similar, but distinct organization) who primarily are travelers who work their way around the country (or countries). They also offer farm exchanges but the focus is not on farming or organic living. With Wwoof, while it is very much a cultural exchange in conjunction with an agricultural exchange, the primary activity is to learn about organic living and growing of food. Therefore hosts just need to be clear and to be aware of the differences when they are corresponding with prospective Wwoofers to ensure that their needs and the needs of the helpers are in synch.

This section presents an overview of a representative number of farms throughout the USA to present a look at the range of options that Wwoofers have to choose from. I have tried to include farms from as many states as possible (forty-seven plus Puerto Rico) and to show the diversity that exists within the WWOOF organization. There truly is a wide variety amongst them, whether we refer to the crops grown and animals raised, the methods used to grow the food, or the size of each farm or homestead, just to mention a few differences. I have intentionally included some that are on the fringes perhaps of what the majority may expect an organic, sustainable farming situation to be.

To begin, Quail Hollow Farm overlooks the Valley of Fire and Red Rocks in a small agricultural community near Lake Mead, Nevada in Overton. This small, family farm is the type that many aspire to for establishing their own small, organic, sustainable farm and the owners enjoy inspiring and modeling their farm to Wwoofers and all interested persons. They have a year round growing season and grow produce for their 150 member CSA which is already in its seventh year. Besides fresh vegetables they have small farm animals including poultry and laying hens, heritage turkeys, and rabbits, an orchard, a greenhouse, an apiary, and their own vineyard. Quail Hollow is not only able to market their products to local CSA members, but they also offer annual events such as "Farm-to-Fork" dinners where everything is prepared from food grown on their farm, and occasionally they even have brick-fired pizza events.

Irish Ridge Ranch, near Half Moon Bay in California, is run by Erin Torney, who markets her food products at local Farmers' Markets. She is in the process of converting the farm from growing field crops to establishing a heritage orchard featuring rare and recovering apple varieties. She also started and now runs two local Certified Farmers' Markets. Erin sells eggs and laying hens, and is active in food systems change, garden based education and social justice issues involving food and food security. Her mixed flock of 100+ rare and threatened breed, laying hens run wild among the beehives, and the flock is fondly referred to as The Farm Fatales. Erin also works in conjunction with many neighbor farms–from first generation farms to those who have been farming for decades, and sometimes there are opportunities for her Wwoofers to continue on nearby farms. Erin wasn't able to write too much about her hosting experience because she is incredibly busy, but expressed that she has enjoyed her experiences for over two years. She came about hosting accidentally, and now has been host for several Americans and Wwoofers from several European countries as well.

Fable Farm in Barnard, Vermont operates a bit differently, cultivating land throughout the town of Barnard. This includes an organic beef farm and another plot of land in the center of their small town that has only one store and no traffic lights. The owner, Christopher Piana, says they are a multi-faceted CSA farm focused on integrating the arts with agriculture. They like sharing their farm with both visual and performing artists while they grow over forty varieties of vegetables, flowers, and herbs for the CSA. They also provide wood-fired flatbread baked in an earthen oven and offer a large variety of fermented food and beverages for sale. Christopher enjoys bringing people together through good, healthy food. In addition to the marketed crops they have beehives, apple and pear orchards, and grow dried beans and corn for their own consumption.

Kathi Whitman owns and operates the Ms Fit Ranch in Liberty, Missouri, not far from Kansas City. Hers is a demonstration farm where she not only grows food with sustainable practices, but also offers classes and workshops on these skills, and has a bed and breakfast on the premises for "staycationers". Her agriculture enterprise markets at a roadside stand and the local Farmers' Market supplying vegetables, fruit, herbs and flowers.

Another multi-faceted farm is the Claymont Community Farm in Charlestown, West Virginia, near Harper's Ferry. This is a non-profit providing facilities for retreats and seminars, where they also provide healthy, nutritious food. The property includes forest, streams, and heirloom orchards in addition to their CSA market garden, areas for raising chickens, greenhouses, and an apple orchard. A strong focus is on agriculture incorporating principles of Biodynamics and Permaculture; they also place high value on community interaction, sharing experiences, and working together.

Super Natural Organic Farms of America, in Ponchatoula, Louisiana, within driving distance to New Orleans, has the distinction of being the first

Aquaponic Farm in the mainland United States to receive USDA Organic Certification through Oregon Tilth in over 3 years. They are very dedicated to increasing healthier farm fishing and to planting fruits and vegetables to alleviate world hunger. Alongside these goals they take a leadership position in the global movement toward sustainability through development and implementation of micro-sustainable aquaponic farm systems for small scale family farms. Additionally they work to strengthen communities, and to improve the air, soil and water in their surrounding area, and increase job opportunities for the Organic Link Farm Network through their educational programs. They seek to train 10,000 family members the skills to farm fish, and to grow fruit and vegetables. The farm follows the practices of natural farming introduced by Masanobu Fukuoka and basic Permaculture principles. *(Author's note: Unusual for WWOOF, where no money is exchanged for services, volunteers here are charged nominal daily fees to cover costs if they stay less than 30 days. Technically they would not be there as Wwoofers until or unless they commit to staying a minimum of 30 days, so this initial period is a non-Wwoofing situation.)*

At a different point in the spectrum of farm experiences is Heartland Farm in Pawnee Rock,

Kansas, which is an 80 acre intentional community and farm comprised of five members of the Dominican Sisters of Peace and two or three rotating volunteers. They raise organic vegetables and chickens, raise alpaca for fleece, and tend their hay fields. They also provide space for retreatants.

North Creek Community Farm is located in Prairie Farm, Wisconsin, quite near an active Amish community and within a couple of hours of the Twin Cities. Their farm has grown and marketed for their CSA for an impressive twenty years and now provides fresh, organic, vegetables, and additionally, herbs and flowers, for 150 members. They strive to make the work for Wwoofers fun and varied and to have clear expectations. (Personally I would like to Wwoof there if only just to experience the Norwegian fjord horses that are used extensively for the farm work!)

One of our neighboring farms on the island of Hawaii is Sambo Berries, a private estate farm with its own waterfall and stream, located overlooking the Pacific. Sam calls it "heaven on earth" where he grows a wonderful variety of great-tasting berries from poha, to raspberry, to blueberry, to strawberry, to the rare thimble berries, all of which he sells "fresh-picked" locally at the Farmers' Market and other island outlets. He grows several other exotic fruits and enjoys providing seasonal instruction on all the various crops to his Wwoofers.

Bobcat Ridge Avocados in Watsonville, California, overlooks the Monterey Bay in Corralitos; Nancy Faulstich and her husband are both teachers. Presently he teaches full time and she is a stay-at-home mom, but together they are developing an organic avocado orchard for future income, with over 200 trees comprised of a sizeable number of varieties,, and they also have a large garden and a variety of other fruit trees to tend which naturally require lots of work. They thoroughly enjoy their Wwoof experiences and provide many opportunities for teaching.

Jason Mc Monagle owns and operates Earthly Elements Farm which is in southern Minnesota, in Madelia. His farm is comprised of 320 rolling acres with forests and creeks located quite near the Mississippi River; he grows his produce, cultivating two acres of mixed vegetable and fruit, selling at Farmers' Markets, and marketing to local restaurants, and the farm is on its way to organic certification. He expressed a bit of frustration, or perhaps just wistful longing, in his comments. In his words: " Being in the center of North America and the main arteries of the continent where rivers flow north to Canada and south to the Gulf of Mexico, one might think that Wwoofers would come by often, but this is not the case. We are on the border of plains, woods, lakes, corn country, the epicenter of agriculture, and worse off yet for today's generation of industrial ag. So I can understand why there has only been one group of Wwoofers to come and that was last year. So my recommendations to myself would be that if I wanted to host more people then I need to move to the east or west coast." I sympathize with Jim and can only guess that more of the volunteers seek both the coastal farms in Hawaii and the Caribbean, perhaps wanting to access beaches along with farms or to have easy access to be able to visit major cosmopolitan cities, but I know that they miss out by not experiencing farms such as his.

Fennario Farms Garden of Life, in Barrington, Rhode Island, is a non-profit operating a satellite system of "urban farms", including over 100 community gardens and a rural farm. They utilize practices of vermicomposting and aquaponics. Wwoofers volunteering here can learn about these types of sustainable growing techniques and also about mushroom cultivation. The staff believes in empowering people through education and collaboration, working to provide opportunities for low-income families or individuals, and for at-risk youth.

Happy Hydroponics in Pukwana, South Dakota has hydroponic greenhouses on their farm near the Missouri River. This family owned and operated venture produces over 70,000 pounds of vine-ripened tomatoes a year and a variety of lettuce, herbs, and wheat grass, in a 100% pesticide free growing environment.

Dropping down to Texas, Wwoofers can find an unusual learning situation which focuses on building sustainable biotech off grid homes. Biotechture Training in Bullard, Texas gives education in building hybrid earthships and aquaponic farms for raising fruit, vegetables, and fish. The system they promote provides shelter, food, water, and power–all the basic needs in one. Their motto is:" Thrive! not just Survive!"

Stoneybrook Organic Farm, near our nation's capital in Hillsboro, Virginia, is a certified organic farm providing food from "farm to table" for several families with their CSA and by marketing directly on their farm. Items available for purchase include humanely raised meat, organic milk, fresh eggs, local honey, and various value-added products produced on their farm or on other local farms. The property contains a heated greenhouse for year-round food production, and for sustainability they use cover crops, compost, and crop rotation.

In Clermont, Wyoming, Prariana Farms sits on the banks of Clear Creek. Wwoofers can participate in helping the owners raise organic heirloom vegetables, from planting, to weeding, to harvesting if they stay for the season. These are then delivered to surrounding communities.

Another non-profit enterprise in an urban environment is Urbiculture Community Farms, this time in a large city, Denver, Colorado. They farm multi-plots of edible landscaping in order to provide nutritious, fresh food to people of all income levels who may purchase on a sliding-scale. Here they accomplish their goal growing sustainable, affordable, local food in a large metropolitan area-again showing us that that not only does food not need to be grown on huge, industrial chemical farms, but not even necessarily in a rural environment. We have the opportunity to provide our own food in every place we live.

In LaBelle, Florida there is a unique farm with a specialty program growing bamboo as a test project. Comfort Edge Bamboo Farm is testing Algae kelp-based nutrients to grow their bamboo. Part of the research explores how kelp being the fastest growing plant in the world, and bamboo being the second-fastest, makes them both key tools for reducing greenhouse gasses. The farm utilizes manure composts, soil bacteria inoculants, and mycorrihizae fungi. Beside these activities, helpers can learn about the production of bio-char which they make in their own kiln, using the organically grown bamboo to capture carbon for the soil.

Hell's Backbone Grill, which is a nationally acclaimed restaurant in Boulder, Utah, is also one of the oldest "farm to table" operations in the United States. Their farm is in a green valley in a remote wilderness area and uses sustainable practices to annually raise over 12,000 pounds of vegetables, to provide their own herbs and flowers, to raise heritage-breed laying hens for their fresh eggs, and to tend and harvest an heirloom orchard for fruit which is also made into jams, butters and chutneys. Everything is served in their restaurant. Additionally, they serve sustainably produced meat provided from neighboring farms.

Another farm in the same area of Boulder, Utah is the Red House Farm, which the owners describe as located in the high desert near the Aquarius Plateau, the highest plateau in North

America. The rural town of Boulder is quite small, but apparently attracts lots of people with its progressive style. Their farm is also small, but very well diversified-- and a river runs through it! They seem to be accomplishing it all raising vegetables and more unusually, heirloom grains, which is not a crop typically grown on most organic farms. In fact they use old style combines to harvest and thresh the grain. Wwoofers will be kept busy in helping with the beehives, tending an alfalfa pasture, and caring for the hens, sheep, pigs, and cows. Red House Farm participates in a CSA and Farmers' Markets where they also sell freshly–baked, soaked-grains bread and are on their way to providing cured meat from their smokehouse. The owners, Scott and Brynn Brodie, are committed to growing with sustainable and organic methods.

Second Chances is a five acre homestead in the Ouachita Mountains of Mena, Arkansas, owned and operated by Jeanmarie Zirger. She is committed to developing a living design based on permaculture ethics of earth care, people care, and surplus care. She is open to community development through consensus decision making, welcomes collaborators seeking to live life abundantly and authentically, and especially enjoys teaching women non-traditional vocational skills, from growing food in the gardens, to tending the laying flock, to building projects. Second Chances is an LGBT friendly farm.

Earthkeeper Farm in Kent City, Michigan is a USDA Stellar Certified organic farm with a focus on quality, efficiency, and production. Their eight acres use Biodynamic principles producing vegetables, fruit, and flowers for their CSA and for selling at the Farmers' Market and to local restaurants. Andrew and Rachelle put effort into nurturing diversity and creating balanced farm ecosystems, believing that building the soil, protecting the land, and teaching new skills helps the success of agricultural enterprises.

While finding organically grown grains among the Wwoof farms is not as typical as finding vegetables or laying flocks, I did find another one - Prairie Rose Organic Farm, in Willow City, North Dakota. This is a USDA Certified Organic family farm where they grow organic grains and keep an Angus herd for meat production sold directly to the consumer–all raised with sustainable practices. For example, they raise all food for the grass-fed herd on the farm, do not use corn or soy, and use prime grazing for their herd.

Traveling to the Rio Grande Valley, in Harlingen, Texas we find A New Earth Farm, which is a self-sustainable farm using organic principles, the Biodynamic methods of Rudolf Steiner, the lessons of Permaculture from Bill Mollison, and living off–grid with solar power and rain harvesting. They do keyhole gardening with raised beds made from tree trunks and have learned methods of raising chickens from Joel Salatin, which they in turn teach, such as using "mob grazing" and chicken tractors.

Back on the west coast is Le Vin Organic Estate Mountain Vineyards and Winery in Cloverdale, California. They are an example of the growing trend in producing organic wine. They grow grapes, fruit, vegetables, and olives to press their own organic olive oil as well as pressing the wine grapes.

Next are examples of farms with their own creameries from different parts of the country. To start with these is Greendale Farm in Madison, Georgia, where they have a farm- to-table enterprise that the owners describe as "from pasture to plate". They produce Certified Naturally Grown beef, lamb, pork, poultry, eggs and cheese, with the creamery producing artisanal cheeses and raw milk. This Certified Naturally Grown designation is about being organic, but they explain that it goes beyond organic in its requirements with rigorous standards, but apparently with less paperwork for the farmer.

The Stone Fox Farm Creamery in Monroe, Maine is in the mid-coastal region of the state. Their main focus is an ice cream making plant with their ice cream produced with local milk and cream from Hilltop Farm. They also source local fruits, and maple syrup for the various flavors. The ice cream is sold at local Farmers' Markets.

Pholia Farm is a solar powered, off-grid goat cheese farmstead in Oregon. They raise Nigerian Dwarf goats with organic and sustainable practices in the Rogue River Valley, teaching Wwoofers both goat herdmanship and cheese making skills. Their farm is a licensed dairy producing handmade, artisan goat cheese from their raw milk. They also preserve meat and can teach butchering skills as well as soap making.

Laurel Valley Creamery in Gallipolis, Ohio operates a grass-fed dairy describing their products as "from grass to cheese" and they use rotational grazing for their herd of Jersey cows producing a large variety of cheeses in this family run farm and creamery.

Reevis Mountain School of Self-Reliance is a more unusual type of organic experience located in Roosevelt, Arizona within the Superstition Mountains Wilderness area. This is a remote wilderness homestead, organic farm, and school that is run by Peter Bigfoot and his wife Patricia. The farm portion consists of a one acre garden for vegetables and herbs, and flocks of poultry-including chickens, ducks, and turkeys. It operates on solar power and water and has no cell phone service for internet access for Wwoofers. They provide a healthy, omnitarian, natural foods diet and teaching about a complete lifestyle including herbology, metaphysics, and wilderness survival. The farm also has a 100 tree fruit and nut orchard and a vineyard and provides market produce sold in the Phoenix area. Herbal remedies are made and sold and the philosophy of natural healing is taught with the philosophy of healing through "herbs, honey, and your hands."

Country Gardens Farm in Yale, Oklahoma lies within the center of the USA in the Great Plains. Neva and Tobie Alsip are intrigued by and are working towards sustainability and self-sufficiency. They are near retirement age with no kids at home. But they do have considerable experience in hosting foreign exchange students, which is akin to sharing your home with Wwoofers. They are a small, family farm with a big garden and several animals and are dedicated to organic principles. They have also taken on alternative construction with a project building a hybrid cob and strawbale structure.

Christie McDowell is from The Good Farm in Berlin, Maryland where they operate a CSA and strongly encourage Wwoofers to go beyond just reading about it and to come be a part of sustainable agriculture. They have diversified learning projects raising vegetables, pork, chickens, eggs, bees, mushrooms, goats, and berries. And for unique interest, in addition to three years hosting Wwoofers, they are also three years into a major project producing a documentary film called *"Building a Living Farm"* which I look forward to viewing. In their words, they are in the midst of "breathing new life" into twenty-five acres of their 600 acre parcel.

The Thankful Goat Farm sits in the foothills of the mountains in Granite Falls, North Carolina. Dawn Mathews says that their goal is to transform their farm into a sustainable one. They have an organic garden, varied poultry, and dairy goats and create value-added goat milk soap and bath products for income.

Shekinah Farm is a small scale, non-commercial homestead on the Tennessee border in Hazel Green, "sweet home" Alabama that seems to have a little of everything needed for a sustainable lifestyle. They grow organic food in raised beds utilizing natural fertilizers from their goats, chickens, cows, and horses. They focus on living and teaching a self-reliant lifestyle -- their primary focus being teaching. Christie Berry also home schools their two children and her husband is a university professor who teaches online courses. Being there one might also learn about such diverse skills as blacksmithing, canning, spinning, butter and cheese making, and other homestead skills depending on the season and what projects are going on. They run a small milk, egg, honey, veggie CSA and a buying Co-op.

Finney Farms, Salmonberry Community Land Trust has yet another different twist to their farm in the Cascade foothills of Concrete, Washington, since theirs is a farm community made up of four households and one shared community house. The efficient farm is rustic with limited running water and uses root cellars versus refrigeration. Besides growing their own organic food they host a buying Co-op, and do trades with a local coffee roaster. They can teach skills for food preservation such as canning and drying since they do much for their own food supplies. They also do home brewing and wild crafting of mushrooms and wild berries in addition to growing their own organic blueberries.

Sassafras Valley Farm, located in in the rolling hills of the Ozarks in Morrison, Missouri, is rather unique, being the only (AWA) Animal Welfare Approved certified goose farm in the USA. They raise goose and ducks for eating, hens for eggs and they provide teaching regarding caring for the land and animal husbandry, including rotational grazing for pastured geese. They use livestock guardian dogs for protection of the animals. Additionally, they make and sell caviar, pastured veal and rabbit, and smoked goose and duck products--unique products not available on many farms.

Farm on Kitchen Branch can be found in the southern Appalachian Mountains very near the Appalachian Trail in Greeneville, Tennessee. Katherine Rollins says they are proud Tennesseans who welcome Wwoofers for a working vacation. Their historic farmhouse has been in their family since 1809. Wwoofers will be learning about growing hay, working in the market garden and with the Farmers' Market, growing corn, and caring for the chickens, cattle, and donkeys. Uniquely they also run a full scale animal kennel facility where they board, rescue, and train service dogs, and they do horse rescues as well.

A bit similar, but perhaps even more unusual than these examples is the McDonald Ranch in Santa Rosa, California. Theirs is a non-profit working ranch serving children and animals. They raise chickens, rabbits, goats, and have several horses, cats and dogs. Their milk is provided from their organic goat herd. Wwoofers learn about animal husbandry-but unlike farms raising animals for food none of the animals raised on this farm are slaughtered or consumed. Children come from after school programs and summer camps and are taught life skills through their ongoing service work helping homeless animals and learning environmental appreciation. They also have established a large garden, growing food for themselves and the helpers.

Back in Petersham, Massachusetts we find a classic New England farm of eighty acres called Sweetwater Farm that has been supplying products for the community for 230 years. The current owners have a very diverse operation where they raise livestock and sell certified organic products such as lamb, broiler chickens, eggs, grass-fed beef, and from the gardens and orchards, fresh fruits and vegetables. On top of that they produce their own maple syrup, grow and sell hay, and make and sell raw wool and yarn.

Red Fern Farm in Gray Court, South Carolina is a small family owned and operated farm that provides an educational experience in a safe, comfortable environment for females only. Meredith Mizell feels that her family can best provide this service by limiting their home to women. Judging by the reviews from their Wwoofers it apparently works out very well. Primarily they grow culinary, medicinal, and aromatic herbs and create value added products, both edible and for the bath. Their major focus is growing and selling their fresh herbs, plants, and specialty produce. Secondly, they raise grass-fed Tunis lamb and market to local restaurants. While they are not certified organic, they use sustainable practices, Biodynamic methods, sheet-mulching and Permaculture principles.

New Earth Organic Farm, located in Colebrook, New Hampshire is part of a twenty-five year old Ecovillage. Their community of thirty five members range in age from seven to sixty-eight. Together they garden their own vegetables, tend their apple orchards, grow various types of berries and raise chickens.

For the Love of Bees is a certified organic farm in the mountains between Taos and Santa Fe in New Mexico. They grow vegetables, herbs and flowers to sell at the local Farmers' Market, but their main occupation is caring for 150 topbar beehives, and they are focused on teaching this particular type of beekeeping. In relation to this task they are creating a demonstration area for honeybee forage species.

In the Little Applegate Hills of southern Oregon we find Wild Wines. This farmstead grows berries and produces a variety of wines made only from flowers, fruits, and berries which they market locally.

In New York state there is Shumei Natural Agriculture which follows the principles of agriculture set up by the Shumei founder, Mokichi Okada. They believe in farming in harmony with nature, without chemicals, fertilizers, or any additives and in this way reconnect with nature through food.

Rather than only producing vegetables or other food, Native Ideals Seed Farm in Montana focuses on saving and marketing seeds. Their farm is organic and raises chickens and eggs and produce. But primarily they grow about forty species of wildflowers on this farm located near Missoula. Wwoofers would help with planting, weeding, harvesting, cleaning and packaging seeds.

Also in Montana, The MPG Ranch in the Bitterroot Valley near Florence is an expansive 8900 acre ranch of rich undeveloped landscape. They strive to preserve its natural beauty and are focused on restoring and protecting the natural diversity. The work consists of weeding out some invasive species and thinning the forest; they also give educational tours. For the food element they tend large kitchen gardens, raise laying chickens, and harvest deer and elk from the ranch.

One rather atypical farm does not produce food as its primary goal, but rather focuses on producing energy-hence the name Energy Farm, located in Oakland, Nebraska. The farm does keep livestock and gardens for food; however, they have converted much of an existing farm for a clean energy demonstration project that is a functional application of energy production and utilization of renewable energy. They employ a combination of solar, wind, methane, biodiesel and gasification in the project.

Michael Walkup runs his farm, Walkup Farm and Heritage Gardens in Crystal Lake, Illinois within commuting distance from Chicago and invites Wwoof participation in the spirit of the original Wwoof exchanges in England where it all started. Sometimes they come for a weekend, or a week, or work during the day but return to their homes in the evenings, since they can commute easily to Chicago, with the train station in walking distance. Conversely many also live on the farm while working, and ideally come for a full season. (But he has also had his share of disappointments with Wwoofers not fulfilling their commitments unfortunately, and his views will be shared in a later chapter.) Walkup Farm provides a unique learning situation with its urban/suburban nature, being a very efficient five acre productive farm in the midst of surrounding subdivisions. They teach a self-sustainable organic lifestyle, growing hundreds of varieties of heritage and heirloom plants as well as several breeds of chickens, ducks, geese, and milk goats.

Farms are incredibly varied in what they produce, how they operate, and in their WWOOF expectations. Some of us are able to grow year round because of mild climates; other farms have short intensive growing seasons. Farms where animals are the primary or sole commodity will operate and need workers year round regardless of inclement or good weather conditions and even those with shorter growing seasons have plenty of preparation and miscellaneous farm chores to be accomplished in the off season.

Pholia Farm is a solar powered, off-grid goat cheese farmstead in Oregon. They raise Nigerian Dwarf goats with organic and sustainable practices in the Rogue River Valley, teaching Wwoofers both goat herdmanship and cheese making skills. Their farm is a licensed dairy producing handmade, artisan goat cheese from their raw milk. They also preserve meat and can teach butchering skills as well as soap making.

Laurel Valley Creamery in Gallipolis, Ohio operates a grass-fed dairy describing their products as "from grass to cheese" and they use rotational grazing for their herd of Jersey cows producing a large variety of cheeses in this family run farm and creamery.

Reevis Mountain School of Self-Reliance is a more unusual type of organic experience located in Roosevelt, Arizona within the Superstition Mountains Wilderness area. This is a remote wilderness homestead, organic farm, and school that is run by Peter Bigfoot and his wife Patricia. The farm portion consists of a one acre garden for vegetables and herbs, and flocks of poultry-including chickens, ducks, and turkeys. It operates on solar power and water and has no cell phone service for internet access for Wwoofers. They provide a healthy, omnitarian, natural foods diet and teaching about a complete lifestyle including herbology, metaphysics, and wilderness survival. The farm also has a 100 tree fruit and nut orchard and a vineyard and provides market produce sold in the Phoenix area. Herbal remedies are made and sold and the philosophy of natural healing is taught with the philosophy of healing through "herbs, honey, and your hands."

Country Gardens Farm in Yale, Oklahoma lies within the center of the USA in the Great Plains. Neva and Tobie Alsip are intrigued by and are working towards sustainability and self-sufficiency. They are near retirement age with no kids at home. But they do have considerable experience in hosting foreign exchange students, which is akin to sharing your home with Wwoofers. They are a small, family farm with a big garden and several animals and are dedicated to organic principles. They have also taken on alternative construction with a project building a hybrid cob and strawbale structure.

Christie McDowell is from The Good Farm in Berlin, Maryland where they operate a CSA and strongly encourage Wwoofers to go beyond just reading about it and to come be a part of sustainable agriculture. They have diversified learning projects raising vegetables, pork, chickens, eggs, bees, mushrooms, goats, and berries. And for unique interest, in addition to three years hosting Wwoofers, they are also three years into a major project producing a documentary film called *Building a*

Living Farm" which I look forward to viewing. In their words, they are in the midst of "breathing new life" into twenty-five acres of their 600 acre parcel

The Thankful Goat Farm sits in the foothills of the mountains in Granite Falls, North Carolina. Dawn Mathews says that their goal is to transform their farm into a sustainable one. They have an organic garden, varied poultry, and dairy goats and create value-added goat milk soap and bath products for income.

Shekinah Farm is a small scale, non-commercial homestead on the Tennessee border in Hazel Green, "sweet home" Alabama that seems to have a little of everything needed for a sustainable lifestyle. They grow organic food in raised beds utilizing natural fertilizers from their goats, chickens, cows, and horses. They focus on living and teaching a self-reliant lifestyle-their primary focus being teaching. Christie Berry also home schools their two children and her husband is a university professor who teaches online courses. Being there one might also learn about such diverse skills as blacksmithing, canning, spinning, butter and cheese making, and other homestead skills depending on the season and what projects are going on. They run a small milk, egg, honey, veggie CSA and a buying Co-op.

Finney Farms, Salmonberry Community Land Trust has yet another different twist to their farm in the Cascade foothills of Concrete, Washington, since theirs is a farm community made up of four households and one shared community house. The efficient farm is rustic with limited running water and uses root cellars versus refrigeration. Besides growing their own organic food they host a buying Co-op, and do trades with a local coffee roaster. They can teach skills for food preservation such as canning and drying since they do much for their own food supplies. They also do home brewing and wild crafting of mushrooms and wild berries in addition to growing their own organic blueberries.

Sassafras Valley Farm, located in in the rolling hills of the Ozarks in Morrison, Missouri, is rather unique, being the only (AWA) Animal Welfare Approved certified goose farm in the USA. They raise goose and ducks for eating, hens for eggs and they provide teaching regarding caring for the land and animal husbandry, including rotational grazing for pastured geese. They use livestock guardian dogs for protection of the animals. Additionally, they make and sell caviar, pastured veal and rabbit, and smoked goose and duck products--unique products not available on many farms.

Farm on Kitchen Branch can be found in the southern Appalachian Mountains very near the Appalachian Trail in Greeneville, Tennessee. Katherine Rollins says they are proud Tennesseans who welcome Wwoofers for a working vacation. Their historic farmhouse has been in their family since 1809. Wwoofers will be learning about growing hay, working in the market garden and with the Farmers' Market, growing corn, and caring for the chickens, cattle, and donkeys. Uniquely they also run a full scale animal kennel facility where they board, rescue, and train service dogs, and they do horse rescues as well.

We may first think of organic farms as an extension of organic gardening, and as you see here, there are many farm members listed which are actually small or large homesteads without commercial operations yet are growing food organically. It is natural at first to envision rows of crops and /or greenhouses with seedlings or full plant production. While that is a large component of the organic farms you will find many variations to this picture. There are farms raising bees for honey and also just for the queens which in itself is a thriving "farm" business; there are dairy farms producing milk, cheese, and yogurt and free-range egg producing farms, and other farms raising poultry for consumption. Ranches raising grass-fed beef cattle, or lambs, or pigs, or other livestock for meat are another option, as well as harvesting wild animals for meat, and related to this but very different still, there are aquaponic farms raising fish in specialized ponds, and still others harvesting fish–or even oysters- sustainably. Another possibility is to learn about raising organic food through hydroponics in greenhouses. Or perhaps the farms consist of orchards with fruit or nut trees that require years of work before harvesting and then continue to produce for many years. I have heard from more than one farm that is transitioning from row crops to establishing heritage orchards. Some farms also incorporate restaurants for" farm-to-table" meals, like Hell's Backbone Grill, or provide fresh produce for local restaurants; this could provide an additional perk for Wwoofers. Several others have bed and breakfast operations and /or farm homestays for the eco-tourists as more people are eager to experience farm life firsthand, even if they are not ready to take the plunge and actually work on a farm. They can teach volunteers about this aspect of the hospitality industry-which in itself is growing as more and more people choose this type of family "staycation", or "eco-vacation" over a more typical hotel stay. Many farms focus on value added production where a secondary level of work is done to create saleable products ranging from olive oils, to jams and nut butters, to dried fruit, and here on Hawaii to vanilla, fresh roasted coffee and now chocolate. *(Author's note: look for bean-to-bar Hawaiian chocolate.)* Farm hosts may educate Wwoofers in selling at roadside stands or at Farmers Markets' stalls providing new skills in marketing. The farms offer such diverse opportunities to learn hands-on and they cover a multitude of areas that comprise the organic community. Hosts provide a wealth of experience to educate the volunteers that are seeking to learn about farming, perhaps as a future work life choice for themselves. In addition to learning how to build soil, plant seeds and propagate plants, there are lessons in mulching and composting, and in general recycling of animal and fish manures to feed the plants. Other farms have more developed systems where they can teach Biodynamic / French intensive farming techniques, and Korean Natural Farming, where one can learn about utilizing the natural indigenous micro-organisms that are in your local environment to feed your soil and plants, and some host farms are teaching Permaculture skills. In many instances hosts are certified in these specific areas and can provide in depth training. Beyond this there is the range of skills for raising chickens and ducks, either with laying hens for egg gathering or for raising organic poultry, as well as raising goats and sheep and pigs and cattle, whether for milk, or for cheese or for meat. A Wwoofer can be taught the intricacies of cheese making at a farm creamery, with a variety of different cheese making processes, or of raising grass-fed beef cattle and what is involved in getting that to market. They may participate in wine making or beer making or mead making, or at least in growing the hops or grapes or raising the bees for the honey! Unexpected skills taught can include root-cellaring and seed-saving; other farms can teach you how to cure and smoke meat, and even how to build a smokehouse may be on the project list. All farms will have endless project lists. Hosts are teaching helpers about the art of fermenting foods such as sauerkraut or other fermented vegetables. I've taught bread baking and jam making on rainy days and I have heard from other hosts teaching these skills too. They may teach you about probiotics and in making yogurt and kefir or kombucha. Not only will Wwoofers learn how to produce food, but in some instances they will gain skills in preparing foods and learn the value of eating healthy, nutritious foods. Many discussions will be held on food! Obviously the major part of the teaching and learning is about growing the food, and then preparing it for meals, but the related educational opportunities are also rich and varied. Alongside growing plants and raising animals farmers are often living off-the-grid and can teach you about alternative energies such as solar power, and wind power. My husband for example teaches the Wwoofers about managing the solar power system, in addition to rainwater harvesting. Farm hosts are teaching sustainable building skills, which may include traditional carpentry skills, or unique alternative building skills such as cob construction, or earth bag building, straw bale construction, or log cabin building techniques. A rancher might teach you about fence repair, or water management, or the ways of establishing healthy watersheds, or a Wwoofer may find himself pitching hay. Activities vary from intensive-grazing management to installing and using drip irrigation, or perhaps something as new as learning to make and use bio-diesel fuel. Volunteers may find themselves cutting firewood for the first time, or learning about something they never imagined such as vermiculture (raising worms for fertilizing and enriching the e soil), or mycology (raising edible and medicinal mushrooms), or perhaps foraging for wild mushrooms, collecting wild herbs, gathering seeds, or learning to make healing herbal tinctures or ointments. Farmers and ranchers will teach the

Wwoofers skills about using and maintaining tools and equipment, which are vital in keeping the farm or ranch running properly, and costly to replace if not handled properly.(Every host probably has a story about improperly cared for tools.)

When Wwoofers seek out farm exchanges, the listings in the directory first give them a clue as to what they will be able to learn. The hosts try to explain as much as possible through the listings, and later through the follow-up correspondence, just what the volunteers can expect. The more correspondence (by e mail, or mail, or phone, etc.) the more they can clarify and paint an accurate picture. Some hosts have begun to use video chat through Skype to truly get a feel of volunteers before they arrive. Often there is much more that cannot even be listed as it varies uniquely with individual hosts. From the very beginning the Wwoof concept fostered cultural interchange alongside the agricultural learning. Building the social interaction skills is something that is learned firsthand, and yet not taught specifically. What occurs is that by participating in a group living and working situations, the skills of interdependence, and working as a team are fostered. Better communication can be built up---of course dependent on how long volunteers participate on one farm. They need to be there a while to find the rhythms and to interact fully. Not all Wwoofers will learn these skills in depth, but for many it will be a first time situation and they are eager and ready to absorb the experience.

The concepts of organic farming and sustainable living are very much about building agriculture skills but also about building community. Wendell Berry has written volumes about these subjects. Some farms may be fantastic at growing food for market, which is a great accomplishment in itself, but it is just as important to have a good community atmosphere and to be teaching this along with the ability to grow food. If not, we revert back to the methods of industrialized agriculture which puts its focus solely on economics rather than community and ecology. Some farms offer even more unusual ways of providing additional benefits and opportunities to learn. For example, there is a farm called Mountain Edible Arts in Burnsville, North Carolina where the owners, Kelly and Jeff are both natural healing practitioners, who collect wild medicinal plants, and have a wealth of knowledge on alternative medicine to share.

There are farms such as LongAcre Creek Herbs in Missouri where the owner, Jim Long, is a national speaker on herbs, and who also writes books and newspaper columns and a blog on the subject, and who, needless to say, has a wealth of knowledge about herbs to pass on to his helpers. His bestseller is _Growing and Using the 10 Most Popular Herbs_ and my personal favorite is _Fabulous Herb and Flower Sorbets,_ just to mention a couple. I corresponded with a unique farm on a small island in Alaska, named Alaska Ridgewood Lodge, where they harvest oysters and the owners Kevin and Lucinda also operate a wilderness lodge. They teach Wwoofers about running the lodge as well as raising oysters. Unusually, I found some farms that in addition to (or even occasionally, instead of) growing organic food, the focus is on turning these organically grown and raised products like goat's milk and herbs and fruits into value-added products such as skincare or body care products, or even cotton or hemp clothing or other household items.

Some Wwoofers intentionally explore farms in the climate they wish to work in the future; others will go out of their way to experience something completely new insofar as climate and /or social experience along with their Wwoofing venture, and still others try to work on several farms in order to explore many options from vegetable growing, to animal husbandry, to living off the grid, and so they will volunteer on farms in several states. Wwoofers have opportunities to discover all the beautiful and different areas of our country and see firsthand how these farms are similar and what distinguishes each one. They may explore very remote farms or the ones that they commute to from a city for as little as a day or a week. Quite a few farms will participate in their local Farmers' Markets, sometimes on a weekly basis, others driving to three or four markets in different locations on different days during the week. A large component of organic farming works hand- in-hand with the "Eat Local" concept and in addition to Farmers' Markets they sustain their farm operations through CSAs-which is Community Supported Agriculture, where people in the neighborhood commit beforehand to purchase shares of local farm-produced food for a set period of time, which can vary from a few weeks to an entire season. This allows farmers to grow knowing they have a market for their food, and in turn the members of their community are assured in knowing exactly where their food has been grown. In both cases it takes a certain measure of worry out of the picture. Farmers arrange for either certain times the members can come pick up their produce, or in some instances make deliveries to the members. Not all of the CSAs are solely for vegetables; they may include, fruit, eggs, dairy, and/or meat or fish, depending entirely on the needs of the members and most importantly what each CSA farm produces. So we can see that the possibilities seem and are endless.

For another example of the diversity, Amy from the Small Family Farm in Sandpoint, Idaho sees her farm as atypical, since they are non-commercial, and grow food just for their family. However, many farms are just that, and often the Wwoofers will seek this type of experience versus one that is more commercially oriented. There is something for everyone. Many of the farms are small family homesteads where individuals take on the task of making their lives more sustainable and are learning as they go. They are also willing teachers, even if their knowledge is limited but they are honest enough to admit they don't have all the answers. Some of these farms are ideal for first time Wwoofers who may not be ready for something of a commercial nature where skills are more critical and workloads sometimes harder. Each farm has unique, valuable lessons to teach and wonderful experiences to be shared. It is important for hosts and Wwoofers to find the right fit for one another. Sometimes it is trial and error, sometimes every exchange works well. Much depends on the attitudes and expectations on both sides of the exchange, and the factors of flexibility, teachabilty, and learnability.

To continue with a glimpse at the farms, Josie from 7B Farm in Petrolia, California on the "Lost Coast" finds her farm, "very attractive to Wwoofers who are questing for paradise," and she isn't surprised that Wwoofers fit in well on their farm and in the tight-knit community surrounding them. She and her husband have raised all five of their kids on farms here and in farms in remote Alaska. Their homes have always provided a very open environment as they welcomed exchange students and visiting teachers and music theater groups. Their kids have moved on to higher education and now live in urban centers in America and Egypt and India, but Josie and her husband have remained steadfast to their ideals of this rural lifestyle, which they chose in the 70s and have not changed their views about.

Another take on the traditional farm is Piedmont Herbs near Chapel Hill, North Carolina. Tony is raising his son there in this intentional community of Blue Heron Farm, and he is grateful for the Wwoofers who add a great youthful spirit and teach him new things too. He used to be frustrated with them for being flighty and non-committed, but he says emphatically, "They are great people."

The Goode Farm quite close to us is owned by our friends Garvin and Laura Goode. They are a sustainable farm that also operates a successful bed and breakfast where their guests enjoy a farm stay complete with farm fresh breakfast, and the experience of the gardens and livestock (while they are not required to participate in the farm work-although some may like to give it a try!) Additionally they raise chicks for breed stock and pullets, selling to others wishing to raise their own laying hens for eggs. On top of that they grow bananas and sugarcane, and make dried bananas and smoothies and cane juice which they sell locally. A large part of their farm was for their CSA supplying wonderful vegetables and herbs and fruit to several local families. They recycle all the manure from the chickens and donkeys for fertilizer for the vegetables and other crops as well as employing the fertilizing system created with their aquaponic fish ponds simultaneously teaching their Wwoofers about "Green Alga Technology" in addition to the other invaluable learning experiences. They also raise pigs, and they have grown great sweet corn to sell at the Farmer's Market. Sometimes they have been able to rely on extended family to run everything with them, but often use Woofer exchanges. They have had some terrific helpers stay long term and like many of us have weathered having no shows and last minute cancellations. But the farm thrives with their own hard work and that of the Wwoofers. They have chosen to be very careful with their application process, checking references, and using thorough screening questionnaires all in an effort to get the more serious Wwoofers who they believe will stick to their commitments and have a good work ethic. They can see some improved results doing all of this, yet as several other hosts have reported there are still no guarantees.

Some farms have one main crop, or it is the sole crop- called monoculture; others can teach biodiversity as they diversify their own farms with an inter-play of crops and/or animals in a balancing act of synchronicity. One thing that all the farms have in common is a desire to grow and produce good, healthy food. The original concept of Wwoof has enlarged in the forty plus years since it was founded by Sue Coppard. As mentioned in the previous chapter, her original concept (and the acronym) was for *Weekend Workers on Organic Farms*, which grew out of her own desire to have this experience and to share it with likeminded people. She quickly found many more individuals with similar desires, who wanted to find out about where and how organic food was being grown, and how it would be to live this lifestyle; and many farms were more than willing to share their ideas in exchange for some extra help.

That eventually grew to become *Willing Workers on Organic Farms* when it went beyond weekends to week long and multiple week adventures. Finally, to go beyond visa concerns and immigration laws, the intent was made even more strongly and clearly that it is strictly an exchange program versus paid labor, and so the name evolved further came to be what we call it today---*Worldwide Opportunities on Organic Farms*. (I understand some organizations still use the previous name of Willing Workers etc.) The concept has expanded to offer even more diverse opportunities as it now incorporates related places to Wwoof that focus on sustainable living, organic restaurants or shops selling organic goods, alternative healing centers and retreats.

There is a myriad of opportunities to practice sustainable living practices. Sustainable growing practices in the production of food are what we first focus on. For example, if we don't deplete the water or the soil resources when we grow, we are using sustainable agriculture techniques. Likewise this holds true if we don't pollute the soil with chemical fertilizers, herbicides, or pesticides. The amount of sustainable lifestyle that goes hand-in-hand with this food production varies from farm-to-farm, but organic farmers by their nature are intrinsically aware of their natural environment and go to great lengths to be ecologically minded and ensure that soil is preserved and naturally enriched, and that water resources are conserved, not depleted. By not using chemical fertilizers the soil is kept intact and improved and water supplies are left safe from harmful runoff. Many farms choose to be certified organic; many others choose to follow organic principles without following the [bureaucratic] and costly process of certification. It's a very personal choice. Often it depends on the market they are trying to reach, or perhaps a farm is not selling any product so does not feel the need to be certified. Still others have turned to alternate certifications such as Certified Naturally Grown which require less documentation, but are still overseen to ensure they meet the specific standards of this organization.

All of the farms offer a diversity of natural beauty as well as a more peaceful, more simple, and typically a rural lifestyle. But you will also find urban farmers producing substantial amounts of food in the cities, and in the suburbs. Family farms may consist of less than an acre or be comprised of thousands of acres, especially if they are raising pastured, grass-fed animals for organic meat. All of these farms are equally valid for the Wwoof exchanges as the common element is growing good food with sustainable, organic practices–whether it be vegetable, fruit, fish, fowl, meat, herbs, dairy, or eggs-and growing it organically, i.e. without pesticides, or herbicides, without relying on chemical fertilizers, and being mindful of soil and water conservation, and regardless of the size of the "farm". Some farms are in transition from former chemical farming to the natural, organic principles they embrace.

Some of the more unusual ones that I encountered during my research include the above mentioned Alaskan Ridgehouse Oyster Farm and Wilderness Lodge, more than one farm that produces herbal wines, and one that is a women owned land that offers a rare feminist setting. (They also host male volunteers.) The manager there shared that a common sentiment they experience from volunteers is "…the amazement of how empowering it is to be in a space with only women, where we are building, and farming, and working hard, and moving heavy objects around…without depending on the muscle or authority of a guy." She recognizes how hard gender roles are to shake even now, and feels they are doing well to help volunteers view themselves in a different way when they leave and learn that they can depend more upon themselves for whatever they need. The idea of self-reliance is something many Wwoofers can take away from their learning experience on the farms. Inevitably while Wwoofing they learn about themselves.

At LoveTree Farmstead in Wisconsin, Mary does a weekly artisan–wood fired pizza. They raise pastured sheep and are known for their raw milk cave-aged cheese (which sounds lovely and especially appealing to me.) In the Sangre de Cristo Mountains in northern New Mexico, Wwoofers stay in a traditional log cabin caring for exotic Goji berries at Taos Goji and they also help with running the eco-lodge. Another atypical Wwoof experience was shared by Helmut from Classic Organic Farm and Market in Gaviota, California. He only has Wwoofers come for one day, for a few hours. The helpers harvest and he is able to show them around the farm. Then he has them help with the easier weeding on the large weeds using hoes. He explains that it doesn't make the work go any faster, but he enjoys the company. At one time he used to have the Wwoofers do the field thinning and weeding, but unfortunately he felt the need to have the work redone by his paid employees. Still he offers a nice exchange for those who are looking for a brief encounter. And as we have learned this method is more akin to the origins of WWOOF where helpers began with just weekend exchanges.

Farmers choose to become hosts with a Wwoof

program for a variety of reasons. In many instances there are well-established farms, already functioning very well with the owners and perhaps paid workers, depending on the size of the farm and if it is or isn't a commercial venture. These farmers may be older, or these farms could be run by relatively young owners who have established their farms early and have maintained and grown their farm operations successfully. They may decide to pass on the knowledge they have gained over the years to a new generation of farmers. In this case they are eager and prepared to teach what they know and are willing and able to provide lodging and meals in addition to their teaching. This type of farm is fortunate in not needing extra hands to run their farm, but instead view Wwoofers as extra help. Most likely they enjoy the intergenerational and intercultural exchanges as well the joy of teaching. On the other hand you will find numerous farms that are likewise well-established, but who find that they really need extra help in order to stay sustainable. They are also willing and able to provide room and board for Wwoof exchanges and additionally are prepared to share their knowledge of farming with these helpers. Often times they will be continually learning themselves, but always willing to teach what they know and learn. They may find that are a bit more reliant on the Wwoof help, and will frankly be in a bind if commitments fall through.

Organic farming is by its nature more labor intensive, and many hands are often needed to make it work. Beyond this there are many newly established farmers and farms who will need help just to get themselves up and running (until they reach the level of sustaining and fall into another category.) These farmers in general thrive on the social interaction and place a high value on the exchange of ideas. For them Wwoofing is absolutely essential and rewarding. Often the farm will be a blend of these elements, perhaps fairly well-established, still needing some help, but primarily self-reliant, yet still enamored with the idea of teaching the concepts they have grown to love and practice regarding organic, sustainable lifestyles and food production. Sometimes the desire for growing organic food outweighs the need or want to earn income, but still requires quite a bit of work to produce. There are of course economic considerations, because whether it is a family homestead or a commercial venture with CSAs or Farmer Market participation, or supplying stores or restaurants where there are costs and balance sheets to account for. By and large you will find the economic aspect is not the first concern, but naturally is a valid concern for each farm.

Scott Brodie of Red House Farm in Boulder, Utah summed up his thoughts nicely concerning the new organic movement and the future of farming in America that he views as still in its pioneering phase. "Sowing seeds for future farmers is probably much more important at this time in history as we need many more farmers out there with the necessary skills if we are going to be able to feed ourselves in the future." He himself appreciates his experiences in the early 90s where he worked and learned on a farm prior to knowing about Wwoofing, and he proudly uses those skills on his farm today.

These next two farms presented here operate quite self-sufficiently. Many farms aim for self-reliance, and of course are using sustainability, but not all are able to be self-sufficient.

The Poor Farm in Gentryville, Indiana is very self-sufficient. On their homestead they raise organic grass-fed beef, which they process themselves into meat, and lunchmeat. They raise fish in their stock pond, and chickens and milk cows; they are able to produce their own butter and cheese besides having fresh milk and eggs, and even make their own soap and laundry soap. Their large garden is 5000 square feet. To continue with sustainable self-sufficiency they run their diesel vehicles on 50% cooking oil. They are clearly able to teach the skills needed for a self-sufficient lifestyle to their Woofers.

Another farm where strong skills in self-sufficiency can be learned is the JCK Family Farm in Scottville, Kentucky, which adjoins a horse-powered Mennonite/Amish community. John Knight began farming his 100 acre homestead twenty two years ago-without the benefit of electricity and he also uses horses for his farming. The family raises cows, and sheep and goats besides the horses, and has established fruit trees and berries. This farm was once commercial, but more recently it has become a subsistence farm for his family where they grow and raise their own food and preserve it. They are able to heat and cook with wood and obtain their water from a cave spring, but they do also have more conventional facilities with running water and power available for the wwoofers.

Rhio's Garden in Eldred, New York is uniquely self-described as a *"truganic"*, Biodynamic, Permaculture farm in the Catskill Mountains of New York State, two hours northwest of NYC. They farm twenty-four acres with about four acres of wetlands, following all the organic standards, and above. As Rhio states "Since organic standards are constantly being downgraded by the USDA", they are not certified organic, but DO NOT use pesticides, herbicides, fungicides, "cides" of any kind, or chemical fertilizers, also following Biodynamic and Permaculture principles. Volunteers help with planting, transplanting, weeding, spreading hay mulch, hauling, fertilizing, harvesting, making biodynamic preps, clearing of brush, stacking of wood logs, rototilling, building fences, pathways, ponds, compost boxes, other building projects, etc. Volunteers also have the opportunity to learn kefir making (both water and milk kefir) with original kefir grains. Rhio is herself a recognized expert on raw foods and a published author of the book entitled _Hooked on Raw_.

Beyond the rich diversity of the farms I corresponded with, I found that they all have a very enthusiastic and positive view of organic farming and sustainable living practices. We all do this by choice, for the principles of organics that we love. Being in touch with the earth, living in beautiful rural surroundings, stepping out of the consumer lifestyle, knowing the source of the food we eat-these are some of the joyful benefits of organic, sustainable living. It may not be a perfect world since naturally it has its challenges, but it is definitely a healthier, natural lifestyle that people consciously choose and appreciate. Along with this I found a nearly universal appreciation for the Wwoof program being utilized on their respective farms and how much it has added to the great environment they already enjoy. They recognize both the value to the agriculture aspect which is foremost, but also for the genuine appreciation for the cultural, social exchange. Even where farms experienced issues with individual Wwoofers, they realized and could appreciate the value of the system. How each farm implements the Wwoof exchanges on their farms we will see has many commonalities, but the experience also differs widely from farm-to-farm due in part to the differences of the farm operations and needs of the farmers. To start with we have seen the farms come in many shapes and sizes, have a wide variety of organically produced food that they are growing for various reasons, and can offer many different views of the organic movement to helpers who come to learn and experience this way of living and growing.

In forthcoming chapters I will explore the hopes and expectations of the host farms, what they offer to the Wwoofers, and the range of living offer to the Wwoofers, and the range of living situations helpers may get to experience. But first we'll continue with some discussion and descriptions of the Wwoofers.

"Eating is an agricultural act."

Wendell Berry

Chapter Three

The Wwoofers

Wwoofers come to us from all parts of the United States and from many other countries around the globe to participate in these farm exchanges. While this book focuses on the farms in the USA, the people helping on the farm bring a huge diversity of cultural backgrounds to the farms. This may provide some challenges with language and perhaps differing ideas in some instances, but mostly it provides a rich environment for cultural exchange, which will be discussed in more detail regarding the benefits of Wwoof Hosting.

So who are the Wwoofers?

Age wise they can be as young as 18, but there is no upper limit. I heard from one farmer who was eagerly expecting a 71 year old helper recently and have heard tales of one only 17 (This would be possible as part of a family exchange since Wwoofers should be a minimum of 18 years old.) We personally have hosted someone aged 60, and since we are in the same age bracket it seemed perfectly normal to us. You will find the vast majority of them are in their 20s and 30s, but age is not the sole commonality.

Most everyone who Wwoofs is seeking an experience, an adventure of sorts, even if farming appears to be a somewhat tame adventure. They will be on their own, but thrown into a new environment, meeting new people of different ages, and backgrounds, including their hosts and their fellow helpers. It can be very exciting, even when a farm is a quiet respite from city life.

Most are seeking to learn something of where their food comes from. The desired depth of experience they want will naturally vary from person to person, but the curiosity is there. Some want to explore the entire food process from the beginning, especially since all they have experienced before is buying groceries in a store. Some want to know the process from soil preparation, to planting seeds, through weeding, mulching, and fertilizing-all the way through to harvesting. Others may just want to harvest and literally enjoy the fruits (or vegetables, or honey, or eggs, or cheese etc.) of the farm! Mealtimes become integral events where the cultural differences become shared experiences along with the food.

The healthy, nutritious meals are often a focal point whether Wwoofers share in meal making or just in enjoying the food. But several hosts have commented on how important providing good food is to the program. They have noticed how much Wwoofers comment on this aspect of their experience, and certainly our Wwoofers can attest to that. Some hosts go as far as saying that the knowledge of better eating habits is possibly an even more important benefit that the volunteers take away with them. After all, they may not all become farmers, but they can all continue in being aware of better nutrition and how to incorporate those concepts into their lifestyle. Still others will seek out farms where they can specifically learn animal husbandry or beekeeping, or any other specific aspect of organic living that they envision needing in their own future.

There is another category of helpers who come because they are at loose ends. Maybe they are just looking for a place to stay for a while, away from their normal routine and home environment. Perhaps travel and adventure is their main priority and they are Wwoofing to enable their travels. Wwoofing certainly does provide a way and means for people to travel relatively inexpensively, working their way around the country (or other countries) on the farms. Others will choose to Wwoof yet actually have no clear idea of why they are doing so.

Different farm hosts will have different requirements they seek from the prospective Wwoofers. The most important qualities are a willingness to work and a desire to learn; and I would safely add good attitude with consensus from the many respondents. No experience is required in general, although again there will be some farms that absolutely need and want experienced help.

The reality is that most Wwoofers do not have experience, which is why they are coming to volunteer. They are eager to learn and experience from the hosts and that is the basic premise. They want to leave behind the hustle and bustle of the large and small cities, to get away for a while from the consumer society, to experience the good life in these more natural habitats-and they are willing to work in exchange for this opportunity to learn.

In our experience with nearly fifty exchanges, my husband and I found very few who plan on becoming farmers in the future. But this has never been a cause for concern. We found most of them to be in between their careers or life paths, often having just completed college, or even fresh out of high school, and wanting this experience before they settled into some more serious study or work. Wwoofing seemed to serve them well to help ground them and give them time and space to consider the next steps on their life path. We've known and shared our farm with future and/or present architects and artists and naturopaths and social workers and even a couple who came to us via Afghanistan and the Sudan and are now doing work with USAID in Southeast Asia.

Jeremy and Julia from Lincoln City, Oregon are excellent helpers with us now, and we are fortunate to benefit not only from the farm work they diligently do, but Jeremy has used his computer expertise to solve a few technological problems on the homestead which we are very grateful for, enjoys cooking, and we enjoy the ease of interaction with them on a daily basis.

Jo is from Ohio and her husband Hubi is from South Africa. After working in Afghanistan, and before they moved on to their next exotic location they were seeking a break from cities and work and wanted to be in a rural, natural environment. So for them Wwoofing was a perfect way for them to accomplish their desire for a quiet, peaceful respite. Fortunately for us they had a great work ethic, were sincere, interested learners, and on top of that were great fun to be with, so it was an excellent exchange lasting a few months.

Jack and Lindsay came to us accidentally. Serendipity often brings the best results in life in my experience, and this case definitely proved true. We had had a cancellation and fortunately for us at the same time our next Wwoofer Kiva, who was on another local farm completing his commitment there, wrote and asked if we had room for two more. It turned out that their experience there was rather lacking in many ways and they very much wanted a change, and their host understood that her small living quarters were not ample enough to provide the best environment for the large number of helpers she had invited at that time, and she knew beforehand that they would be leaving. (I hasten to add that it is only fair to check with the host when you are accepting new Wwoofers who are leaving a neighboring farm. First, it is a respectful courtesy; secondly, you may learn something about your prospective helpers.)

After inviting them to visit our farm, which we are not usually able to do first; we instantly knew it was a good match. The next several months with the three of them turned out to be a fantastic Wwoofing experience and we still miss them. And that spring we were up to four helpers at one time (which we have only done rarely) since we also had Sean who was another great complement to our community.

They each had an excellent work ethic, enjoyed being outdoors rain or shine, never complained, and appreciated the prepared meals as well as participating in making some great ones doing some excellent cooking of their own for all of us. They were intelligent and communicative and mature and fun to be around. What more could we ask for? The fact that they didn't go on to be farmers is irrelevant, although Jack and Lindsay do work on their own garden plot in a community garden in Portland.

Lindsay is now on her way to becoming a Doctor of Naturopathy, Jack is completing his Masters' degree and caringly runs a Social Youth Program, Kiva is studying Biophysics, Sean is a writer, living in California, Jo and Hubi are currently living and working in Myanmar with USAID – enthusiastic, eager, hard-working ex-pats, and we are as proud of each them as we are of our own kids and we not only stay in touch but visit them and vice-versa. So if I sound like someone bragging about my kids…

And speaking of the serendipity factor-we went against our preferences for singles vs. couples and against our preference for no more than three helpers at a time, yet our instincts to ignore our own biases worked out strongly in our favor.

Other volunteers have been office workers or waitresses, not settled in a career yet, and at the time just looking for an utterly different environment temporarily; still others have been serious travelers just passing through. We have also experienced drifters who don't have a clue why they are here, or where they are going, but chances are there will always be a number of those who are also Wwoofing.

For example, Sarah was in between college and figuring out how to move permanently to live and work in France. Dan came to us after a short time at a monastery and is now living in a Zen monastery long-term. Regarding the few others who were just drifting, hopefully Wwoofing impacted them in a positive way fostering social and cultural exchanges that will affect their future situations.

Mostly we've had fascinating, interesting exchanges with young people from all walks of life and several have become lifelong friends. Among our neighbors hosts have exchanged with future and former Peace Corp workers. Some farmers have had Wwoofers who they later have hired to stay on in paid positions. I was at a baby shower not long ago for a young woman who met her then future husband while she was Wwoofing.

A few happily have gone on to start urban organic gardens with the basic principles they learned, or to continue ones they had before coming to the farm. Often the ones who come with zero experience turn out to be the very best of workers. They have usually been so delighted to be out of the classroom or out of a cubicle that weeding, tedious as it can be, turns out to be invigorating and satisfying. (It has also helped that the view while we work is one of whales breaching in the Pacific in the winter and just plain beautiful the rest of the year.)

On the other hand, occasionally you may find someone who believes he or she knows more than you do, despite limited experience, and so it may not always be an advantage to have an experienced "farmer." Some hosts have shared that they have encountered contentious personalities who if they had the slightest bit of experience either would not follow directions from the host, or worse, insist they know more than the host, even if or when the hosts had been successful farmers for many years! But in our experience, and again with reports from many farmers surveyed, it seems that often the ones who come with a bit of background and experience, coupled with the desire to learn and a healthy work ethic were among the very best of Wwoofers.

There are arguments for both sides. I've had hosts say they prefer the non-experienced helpers because they have a blank slate to work with where they can teach the methods needed on their farm, which could in fact differ from another farmer's ideas. In particular, this works great if the volunteers are also the teachable type.

On the other side of the equation hosts would argue that they tire of teaching new helpers how to do basic chores of using simple hand tools or pulling weeds, therefore they really appreciate the volunteers who have these basic skills as it frees them up to teach more interesting nuanced skills-perhaps propagating seedlings, or grafting trees, or even cheese making or preserving food. But most everyone has to start with basic everyday chores and usually this involves the simplest routine tasks and in general the Wwoofers are eager to learn and pitch in well, even if some need more instruction and looking after initially.

Many Wwoofers manage to delightfully surprise the host by being especially enthusiastic and willing and ready to learn all they possibly can. And this coupled with some basic skills they already have makes for an excellent opportunity for the hosts and Wwoofers to work together. There is still teaching and learning, but at a level akin to an advanced student in school versus a beginner.

An ideal Wwoofer is not only willing, enthusiastic, and teachable, but loves sharing ideas and participating in the challenges on a farm and even brainstorming to solve problems. This type of person doesn't just sit and wait for instructions, but jumps in when he or she sees something that needs attention. Of course, not overstepping that boundary and not making decisions that could impact the farm by creating a new problem inadvertently is the key to success. Here again several hosts concurred that they have been fortunate to have Wwoofers just like this and were very grateful.

For example, we had the pleasure of hosting one very intent young man who is serious about farming, but simultaneously lighthearted and thoughtful, as well as thought provoking in the best sense. He was a part of our family for over five months and has plans to start his own sustainable community one day. Trent had some farming experience having grown up in a very large family in rural Iowa, and reads voraciously taking in knowledge from every available means. He intends to incorporate organic farming and sustainable living fully into this lifestyle. His plans include building sustainable housing; recently he wrote and shared that he completed a workshop on Earth Bag Building. He intends that every aspect of his farm community will follow the guiding principles of sustainable, organic living.

He was perhaps our most serious helper, fully embracing the world of organic farming, always reading and learning in his spare time, (that is when we weren't working or sharing meals or sharing ideas together ourselves), and always with an outstanding attitude and sense of community. We shared countless discussions and ideas and the memories are wonderful. Perhaps we will Wwoof on his farm one day.

Regardless of the backgrounds or experience, each Wwoofer brings his or her own stamp to your farm. Rob of Sun One Farm in Bethlehem, Connecticut shared what he views as the different types of Wwoofers he has experienced. He expresses a difference between American and European helpers. He has found that the U.S. workers are generally in their 20s and early 30s and mostly searching, seeking, and figuring out what they want to do with their lives. Agriculture, and learning about it, is purely secondary. He found himself taking on the role not only of a teacher but also as that of big brother, and mentor, and friend, even as a substitute, temporary step-dad, all of which was demanding but rewarding.

On the other hand, in Rob's observations, the European and Canadian helpers in the same age group that he had on his farm tended to better workers, were more worldly, and were utilizing the Wwoof program to see the USA. But as he sees it they needed little hand-holding, being already used to traveling and living away from home and on their own. He concluded that having a mix of both types on his farm was ideal. In his words, "I am honored to be a Wwoof host and know that as long as I own the farm Wwoofers will continue to be welcome here. I like to think that this experience helps them and I know it gives me great satisfaction. Many times when they leave it's like a parent sending their kid away to college, and I miss them."

Dave and I have shared the same sentiments

with many of our Wwoofers. Fortunately, with Facebook and email many are good about staying in touch, and we do continue to be friends with many of them and enjoy visiting them when we are able to travel.

Rachel from Casarosa Farms had this to say: "We have the best luck with travelers and people from abroad. Many of the Wwoofers that indicate they are specifically interested in learning how to farm are often the ones that have the worst work ethics, the strongest opinions, and the most abrasive personalities....but overall, we have never had a Wwoofer that I would say was a bad person. They have all been wonderful giving individuals, with things to learn and things to share."

Kate Stout from North Creek Community Farm in Prairie Farm, Minnesota has had helpers for over ten years and they have come from Europe and Asia and from all over the United States, varying in ages from 16 to 52. She had this to say about hosting her helpers: "When Wwoofers arrive on the farm a renewed sense of energy enters us all." She goes on to describe how after a brief awkward period of settling in they enthusiastically join the crew with the farm tasks. What works best for her farm are short stays from one to three weeks. She loves interacting with each new volunteer, she keeps a memory book of comments and pictures, and happily has remained friends with many of her former volunteers. She recognizes that they all have provided not only help but interesting learning opportunities for her as well as them. They discuss politics, and religion, and the world at large. She fondly remembered in particular one summer hosting a Christian Rastafarian musician at the same time as two Jewish high school students from New York. Kate concludes her remarks with this, "No one has ever taken advantage of my generosity and I look forward to more contact with the world and the USA through the Wwoofer program."

Other hosts have talked about how so many diverse Wwoofers will easily manage to get along well with one another, and are able to easily fit into the new household situation in most cases. These instances of bridging the gaps of age, and ethnicity, and race, and gender, and the fact that they were city-dwellers before this moment, always brings heartwarming satisfaction that the cultural exchange is working so well.

Bev Rutter responded to me from her farm, the Prairie Flower in Spencer, Iowa with a bounty of positive comments as her experience with Wwoof has been stellar. (And the review comments from her Wwoofers are equally impressive.) Their farm is an entire section of land and grows native plants and grasses for their wholesale and retail nursery, and a river runs through it. Theirs is a multi-generational family business where the kids and even grandkids are involved. "We have had wonderful Wwoofers!!" says Bev, "all a little bit different, wonderful, nonetheless."

She is appreciative that they sometimes work in adverse conditions and do not complain. It must be enjoyable on her farm for the Wwoofers as she says, "some return for visits and also to hone their skills."

Over the five years they have been hosting she says they treat their helpers like family and in turn they have found them all to be pleasant and easy to accommodate. She believes they take away good memories. For example, some of the helpers come to her from the west or east coast and this is usually their first time experiencing a "whole sky sunset" or lightning lighting up the entire sky, and seeing the whole milky way of stars—things that Midwesterners take for granted. She enjoys introducing them to such novelties as the world's largest county fair, (where they can also indulge in a Midwest county fair staple-namely Tom Thumb donuts).

Amusingly she tells of how her own children were worried for them when they first started hosting-warning them of letting in strangers and the likelihood of the TV going missing-but they stuck to their own instincts and have proved the opposite. They often recommend Wwoofing to others since their experience has been so positive. And judging by their Wwoofer comments it is clear that their volunteers leave quite satisfied and with great memories.

Genie from Spencer Creek Range near Eugene, Oregon shares that she was so busy, she wasn't quite sure how to keep the myriad of farm related activities going until that fateful day that she discovered the Wwoof program.

The farm is a "back to the land" project with milk goats, chickens, and a big garden, but she also started a local Farmers' Market, and she and a woman friend serve locally grown food at a restaurant there during market hours; additionally she has a commercially certified kitchen, and she has spearheaded an effort to upgrade the grange, as she is also a political activist and she is also a teacher. A very busy dedicated woman!

The first helpers they brought on were a couple taking a break from college. Genie says, " The Wwoofers have helped in every way possible, first running around cleaning up after me, and then breathing life into the garden." She delighted in their help weeding, and clearing paths, and tending the garden and goats lovingly. Her husband was able to teach some carpentry skills, and in return their Wwoofer Rob was able to teach her husband Glenn how to use some of his own tools, and Rob even helps out by selling produce at the market, while Rachel helps at the market café.

She dreads the thought of them leaving, which inevitably they must, and she knows they will miss their Wwoofers terribly, but look forward to staying in touch, and hopefully finding more that will also fit in so well. Her first contact with Wwoof was so positive, she is buoyed by the idea of continuing, and this too is true from many hosts across the country.

The Wwoofers leave indelible marks on the farms, the homes, and the people they interact with in the hosts' families, and also with their regular employees in many cases.

Roy Stamey from 20 Mile Farm in Two Rivers, Alaska shared his wholehearted support of Wwoofers, even though they are relatively new to farming. Amusingly, the one surprise they had was when their Swiss female Wwoofer arrived at the train station; she came with four large suitcases which barely fit in his SUV. But more importantly they found her to be "a wonderful worker, and also very pleasant to share meals with."

Annie from Bright Hope Farm in Hughesville, Missouri has had eight Wwoofers come over the course of the last year and says overall it has been a great experience, with the good far outweighing the bad, which echoes many Wwoof host sentiments regarding their Wwoofers.

She found they especially wanted to learn about where their food came from–realizing full well it doesn't come from a grocery store shelf, but being in the dark about the realities. They know when they purchase food it is so altered from the original product on the farm that "they want to experience the food process from the beginning." She finds some Wwoofers "who want to learn everything –not just growing food and raising animals, but also frugal living, and eco-friendly living, alternative energy, and sustainability in the hopes that they can put these into practice one day on their own place."

Annie really enjoys these people who are so eager to learn, and she thoroughly enjoys sharing her extensive knowledge.

From Heartland Farm, Sister Terry kindly corresponded with me about the sisters' experiences with Wwoof hosting which she says have all been positive and unique. They have hosted volunteers from various organizations before, but find the Wwoof volunteers to bring the best experience. She says, "Folks who come here are really looking for ways to live more sustainably on this Earth, and this is so important to us as well." They have hosted Wwoofers with ages ranging from 19 to 61, and stays vary, lasting from two weeks to five months; these included several single participants and a married couple.

Chillys Case has a market garden farm, located in Glade Spring, Virginia, specializing in black raspberries from a huge patch and his favorite-fingerling potatoes. He shares some of his thoughts from an adventurous five years hosting his Wwoofers at the Case Country Road Farm.

Above all he has learned to be patient. He recognizes that they truly want to learn –more often than not with enthusiasm and excitement, but that they basically come with no prior knowledge, so he is there to impart those skills. He, like many hosts, has sometimes to remind himself of this-hence the comment on patience. While he has seen the spectrum from hard workers to lazy ones he believes most of them are "free spirits and easygoing". He has had one Wwoofer work out so well he has been able to hire her on as employees after the Wwoof commitment was completed.

Perhaps the worst Wwoofer he hosted the one was who exhibited absolutely no interest in being there-presumably talked into it by his dad. Chillys tried to get him motivated and as he always does invited questions since he enjoys teaching and sharing what he knows. But this particular helper who had only been there a few days stated remarkably that no, he had no questions, he had seen enough and knew how everything worked. He also stated how he had no idea how hard farming was, which for many of the volunteers is true. However, most hosts add that even those who express that still pitch in enthusiastically, unlike this lone example.

In concluding comments, Chilly shared that he truly loves the Wwoof concept and appreciates having them on his farm. "Like many small farmers, I could not do what I do in the amounts I want to do without them." He also noted that recently there has been more stiff competition among the hosts in the region to get enough Wwoof help, which he attributes to the economy.

Several hosts shared how they also appreciate it when their Wwoofers have enjoyed total immersion in the entire lifestyle of the farm and family, not having the end of interest and learning coincide with the end of the workday, or with working with the plants and animals. They report very satisfied helpers who express gratitude for being accepted as part of the family and appreciation for hosts who are passionate about their own lifestyles and the farms they operate.

Annie, from Bright Hope also asks each of them about their previous Wwoof ventures, so she herself can learn from their suggestions for improving, and invites suggestions from them for fun projects to do.

It seems true for many of the contributors that this open door, or revolving door of information exchange is a great benefit. New hosts, or ones who are still wondering whether they should open their farms to Wwoofers will be pleased to know that not only will they learn as they go, but they will get many tips from their Wwoofers, especially if they select ones who have previous Wwoof experience.

Some hosts talk about how interesting it is

meeting Wwoofers who are stepping out of their chosen paths of continuing education and careers to experience these authentic lifestyles that put them in touch with the real world. They learn to work with others, and to interact in meaningful ways and when they stay any length of time, they can observe the growth in the Wwoofers.

One Wwoof host, Josie at 7B Farm, shared her experience with two friends who traveled together to Wwoof after completing their first year at Gallaudet University in Washington, D.C. which is a school for the deaf. Josie and her husband delighted in watching them going up and down the rows together weeding and signing.

Jim from Long Creek Herbs in Blue Eye, Missouri contributed some of his hosting experiences and the variety of Wwoofers he has hosted. He had already had previous experience hosting international students for eight to nine months at a time. He has had Wwoofers come for short stays of a couple of weeks to learn herb growing and cooking, others who come for extended periods of time, and also one who returned for several seasons because he himself recognized, "There is too much to learn in just one season."

Jim goes out of his way to inquire specifically

of the applicants about what they would like to learn. He considers his garden his own special paradise, and he wants to know as much as possible about who will be working with him. Some want to get beyond their comfort zone, others are too new to this to even know yet.

Some other Wwoofer examples from Jim include a couple in their late 40s who came as part of their vacation (his oldest helpers to date), and the case of one who worked very hard to reach their remote farm. This Wwoofer, Seth, must have been very determined; he arrived two months late after having his expensive bike and all of his gear stolen in another state, and had to work to replace them before continuing on his journey. He was industrious too and "set to work immediately upon arriving."

Jim says, "Each brings his or her own set of skills, questions, and experiences." When they share meals they use the time to visit and get to know the volunteers better, and hear their thoughts. He continues, "This is one of the great joys of the Wwoofing experience."

In every instance they have continued their friendship and connections to their Wwoofers. But he has chosen his Wwoofers carefully. He also had some unusual requests from would be Wwoofers at his farm who were completely off-track about communicating, let alone making a commitment. But again, he chooses carefully and never has problems with his helpers. Most hosts stay in touch with the ones that have turned out positive-the majority certainly-but not automatically inclusive of all.

Nancy from Bobcat Ridge Avocados kindly contributed many thoughts on her and her husband Kenneth's interactions with Wwoofers. She begins, "Hosting Wwoofers has allowed us to almost keep up with the basic maintenance of the grounds, and move ahead on some projects that had been in the background. The helpers have not only planted, weeded, mulched and harvested the garden, but they have done various tasks including research and building barn owl boxes, and even providing a variety of foreign-language tutoring, and informal teaching of art and music and dance. The most valuable aspect of hosting Wwoofers has been the chance to create a larger community around us."

Nancy enjoys having dinner guests every day who volunteer in a wide variety of ways, which supports their lifestyle, ultimately benefiting every member of their family. Their four year old especially loves the regular attention and interaction, and the adults love the exchange of conversation and ideas, and see that they are also developing a wide network of friends. They inquire about what Wwoofers want to gain from their experience and try to cater to their interests.

She finds it "a joy to cook for such an appreciative audience," and adds, "it's been wonderful to share not only our home and food but our whole lifestyle with people eager to learn from us." Nancy shares the mutually appreciated benefit that many hosts express-hearing stories from people from other countries-traveling vicariously as some say. It is also enlightening to interact with people much younger than themselves which is often a teaching experience in itself on the art of conversation.

Nancy likes that the helpers somewhat validate the lifestyle they are living by openly admiring the way they live a sustainable, low-impact lifestyle. The helpers gain the practical sense of how much work goes into growing food. In their experience just about everyone who has done exchanges with them has fit in very well with one exception, and that taught her" how to follow her instincts more, and to check in periodically with Wwoofers' experiences, and to always clarify our expectations as hosts."

The diversity of ages, religious beliefs, political views, ethnicities, personalities, goals, life experiences, family backgrounds, not to mention the degree of independence and self-awareness that each Wwoofer brings will vary considerably. But inevitably they will amaze and surprise you and enrich your farm in ways you don't even imagine beforehand.

Basically they are seeking to experience the lifestyle within the organic movement, with a firsthand knowledge of what it takes rather than to be an observer. They want something meaningful, much more than to just be on a vacation. Ideally the farm hosts offer some training in rural living and provide a safe, welcome environment that puts Wwoofers in touch with nature. The work provides physical exercise beyond the exposure to farming and agriculture Most importantly we all get to interact with people of different cultures, backgrounds, and ways of life.

Micah Foti from Ajila Ama Farm in western North Carolina was delighted to share his first ever Wwoof exchange. "Our first two Wwoofers are here now and things are going great. Understandably I was a little apprehensive at first, inviting strangers into your home and into your life is a big step. What if they get angry and destroy something like my barn or an orchard? What if they are thieves and load all my power equipment into their car and flee in the night? All these things were unfounded of course, however I couldn't help but worry a little bit. I am not a person who believes in locked doors and gated fields, so the more trusting side of me won out in the end and we invited some wwoofers into our lives. So far..........so......good!

I truly wish that I had heard of WWOOF when I was a little bit younger and less anchored, Wwoofing would have been invaluable for me to learn some of these practices before I dove in headfirst and started our first blueberry orchard. I try to point out my own mistakes to anyone who seems interested in starting a blueberry farm, so hopefully theirs will be better than ours. I just wish someone had done that for me, or I had the opportunity to learn from another farmer.

Knowing that these types of organizations exist is really great and I hope that we can not only receive some help but also help someone else who may be thinking of just starting out.

The help that WWOOF has brought us so far has been awesome. Having these guys around has been awesome. They of course don't know everything, and I find myself having to show them things that I take for granted that the knowledge is 'general knowledge' but it's important to realize that people live different lives and that we do not all acquire the same knowledge. I suppose that's part of WWOOF though, the information sharing between two parties and the shared life experiences coming together. So far I am really loving WWOOF and we have plans to build several structures for temporary communal living based around WWOOF and other similar organizations. I am thankful for all the work getting done and am more thankful for the boost to motivation that I have received, as I truly feel the biggest help has been that having these guys around is more of a boost to myself to get up and accomplish things that I have been putting off while they are here."

David Kendall of Trout Lily Farm, coincidentally also in North Carolina, has hosted Wwoofers for a little more than a year and is already up to about thirty to date. To summarize his overall Wwoof experience he said, "They have been GREAT help for all aspects of our operations which includes hospitality, forest management and growing food. They are all seeking ways to 'survive' the industrial world-either on their own, in communities, or just looking for alternatives." When he wrote they had eight female Wwoofers where normally they host no more than five. But he added," These gals are really great. They are from: Arizona, Canada, California, North Carolina, and Illinois."

Carl and Lorna from Twin Brook Farms have been hosting on their older family farm impressively since 1970, even before the WWOOF USA program was started here. They have enthusiastically hosted as many as 33 helpers in one year. They proclaim Wwoofers as coming from the Butterfly Clan. Lorna explained it this way:

"They float and fly, landing on the farm with their beauty and skills, sharing with the Twin Brooks Farm, and then they fly off to take their loveliness and hard work to others."

They added this advice: "Do not neglect to invite strangers into your home lest they be angels unaware. *Sic* [Paraphrased from Hebrews.]

And in closing they summed it up beautifully by concluding,

"We have hosted hundreds of angels."

"A civilization flourishes when people plant trees under which they will never sit."

Greek Proverb

Chapter Four

Connecting Hosts and Wwoofers

Even though commercial, industrial farming still constitutes much of the agriculture in our country in this century (and as it has for quite some time); fortunately there are many thousands of small organic farmers across our country. A tiny percentage, yes, but the organic movement truly is a growing one. Out of these well over a thousand participate in the Wwoof USA program. [Actually there are close to 1600 to date that are current members.] Additionally there is a distinct organization of WWOOF HAWAII which lists approximately 200 farms just within our islands.

Farms freely join the WWOOF USA and HAWAII organizations for a nominal fee; the hosts provide a detailed listing describing their farms to be entered into the online directories (and print directory for WWOOF USA), describing what they are looking for in Wwoof exchanges, and what they offer to the helpers in exchange. Wwoofers with paid membership can then search the farm listings for places where they would like to work and learn, and then write to the hosts to inquire about space and suitable times. Sometimes hosts will look through member listings and their profiles and contact an individual offering him or her an opportunity to exchange on their farm. In general, however, it is the Wwoofers who initially contact the hosts.

So Wwoof hosts and Wwoofers connect through the member listings. It starts off innocently enough with an e mail or in some cases a phone call. As the process continues hosts choose to offer space to prospective Wwoofers in many different ways. Ideally, the Wwoofers who wish to come have read your listing thoroughly, address your requirements, and write about how they would like to participate on your farm. In this way the host can begin to assess how good a match this may be. There will be follow-up e mails and/or phone calls and arrangements are made that presumably are acceptable to all.

Many of the farms are small family homesteads where individuals take on the task of making their lives more sustainable and are learning as they go. They are also willing teachers –even if limited but honest enough to admit they don't have all the answers. Some of these farms are ideal for first time Wwoofers who may not be ready for something of a commercial nature where skills are more critical and workloads sometimes harder. Each farm has unique, valuable lessons to teach and wonderful experiences to be shared. It is important for hosts and Wwoofers to find the right fit for one another. Sometimes it is trial and error, sometimes every exchange works well-depending on the attitudes and expectations of both sides and the factors of flexibility, willingness to learn, and "teachabilty."

From our personal perspective we like to have a beginning and end date that a helper would be willing to commit to for their exchange, so we can plan on other helpers either before or after and coordinate dates. I found clear consensus on this point when inquiring with other hosts. This seems very straightforward, but in actual practice does not always work out. Communication becomes a critical component in having successful matches.

If there is one mantra I heard expressed more than others from the numerous hosts who contributed their ideas, it was the one stressing clear communication. The Wwoofers deserve and need to know what is expected of them, and the host deserves and needs to know what to expect from the helper who will come live on their farm. Naturally, there will be much left unsaid out of necessity, and one can never know before actually meeting one another, and most likely even working and living together a bit, before knowing just how well it work out.

Most of the time in our experience, it has worked out beautifully.

We find the screening process for us works out best using intuition combined with what they say and write. When we (rarely) did not follow our instincts, when we felt there were red flags for example, but erred on the side of "needing" help it hasn't turned out ideally to say the least; but otherwise most often this method has served us well. And once again I found much agreement on this statement. We don't use a written application with specific requirements. For us if someone conveys a genuine interest in sustainable living and learning about organic farming, and if they are prepared for a quiet communal type of social life with other Wwoofers and ourselves to some degree that is sufficient to give them an opportunity. But we write several times usually, and we use phone calls, and read their profiles and ask questions. Some hosts use Google to research, and some use Skype to have face-to-face contact.

Several hosts, including myself, have expressed that despite the explicit advice on the Web site to write personal letters after reading the listings carefully (and the urging to them to honor their commitments) it is easy to spot when they haven't even read your listing and are just sending out mass generic mailings like darts, just hoping one will stick. We definitely prefer and need people who can communicate well when here, so it is a fairly accurate indication of how their communication skills will be on the farm if they read diligently and actually address what you have stated in their listing. You can usually conclude they will be good communicators when working with you and that they are good candidates from the start.

Other hosts are learning how important it is to read the profiles (although regrettably many of the Wwoofers inexplicably do not post one) and to follow up with the above mentioned checking Facebook, or Google etc. to get a better of idea of whom you will be hosting.

We used to respond to every single letter at length and still do to anyone we can easily determine has at least read our listing which is very detailed. We no longer respond to general, vague inquiries, simply because we would not like to host someone who didn't express an interest in knowing about the farm they were coming to live and work on. If the listing states that the farm has no openings for September and they ask to come specifically in September, it simply doesn't go any further for us.

I found many hosts who share this philosophy. And we each continue gladly to correspond at length with the ones who are genuinely interested, even if all them do not end up coming to our farm. Answering questions and alleviating their fears or their apprehensions beforehand is part of the process. We want to assure that they know they will be coming to a welcoming, safe, secure, and stable environment.

Other farms find an application for screening to be absolutely essential for a part of their process of choosing Wwoofers. Meredith, the farm manager at Red Fern Farm in Gray Court, South Carolina shared their farm's process. She says that not screening enough taught them some hard lessons, so as a result they have implemented a thorough application for screening. And as a result of this screening they have welcomed and hosted many eager, enthusiastic, hard-working young people on their farm.

What she and many hosts look for is for is that Wwoofers are passionate about growing versus just looking for a place to stay. Hosts find it necessary to make their expectations clear. For example, letting them know the work can often be hard, and monotonous, and the weather conditions may not be ideal, but they will be expected to work nevertheless, is fair and important to mention before they agree to come.

Our neighbor Garvin from the Goode Farm also believes in a thorough application as part of the weeding out process and he sees how it eliminates the lazy ones easily. The ones who go through the process willingly take it seriously and that is what he is looking for. He has a wealth of knowledge to share in many aspects of farming and he wants to share it with willing workers who genuinely want to learn.

Another point that invariably hosts have agreed on is the importance of stressing the degree that the farm will be dependent on their word and commitment to specific times. In most cases farms who have last minute cancellations find it very stressful; not only are plans for projects stopped in their tracks, but it is distressing to know you have turned away several prospective helpers for the same time period-as we never considered overbooking-and now have no help and no time to find an instant replacement. This point will also be discussed in more detail in a later chapter, and is the only real negative we personally have experienced with the entire Wwoof experience. And this appears to be true for all of the Wwoof hosts I have been in contact with very minor exceptions.

Hosts use different methods for their screening process and naturally differing applications with questions that are relevant for them. La'akea Farm has found their written application to be very effective. They ask detailed questions about prior, practical experience and also about the applicant's self-awareness, and they request professional references. They prefer Wwoofers with a background in farming and Permaculture

In fact, as they also have people who come and pay to learn as interns, they will often suggest this as a preliminary to volunteering as a Wwoofer on their farm. They learn quite a bit from the application responses and the responsiveness of the applicant and use this to discern who they invite to participate. They can gauge how genuine the interest in farming is and how much the applicant wants to learn about sustainability and island life, and which skills and energy they will be able to contribute in return for their accommodation and food and learning experience. They agree to a one month exchange with

125

a review process after the initial two weeks.

Other hosts have a similar application with questions, although some do so to a lesser or greater degree of detail. Some host farms are very specific about who they invite for exchanges. Janelle from Hard Cider Homestead in Ringoes, New Jersey says that their Wwoof experiences have all been very positive, and she attributes that in a large part to their careful screening process. They have decided to only accept female volunteers who are under 30 years old on their farm. She feels they can more easily provide a safe, comfortable environment for their helpers this way. She also finds females to be better house guests. She first makes it clear in the written correspondence what the expectations will be and what they offer, and then follows through with a phone interview before hand. She likes being able to speak directly to the women and explain even more clearly what has already been discussed in writing. When they arrive she again sits down with them for open communication, so everyone is clear , and she encourages open communication at all times, wanting them to be open to approaching her with any concerns that may arise or if they are uncomfortable with anything.

Emily Beltzer is the farm manager in Prescott, Wisconsin at The Borner Farm Project. As a new host she was very willing to share their first Host experience. She provides the story of how they went about starting on their Wwoof journey writing the following:

"Before registering as a WWOOF-USA host farm we did our research! We read about the positives and negatives of being a host farm. We read horror stories from farmers and Wwoofers alike that made us want to run the other way. We read accounts from both sides that said joining the Wwoofing community was the best thing they could have done.

We are not afraid of risks at our farm. This opportunity had potential. We would try it, see how it worked, and discuss results. And lo, not long after registering as a host farm, we were contacted by Nancy and Andrew, wondering if they could spend a week at our farm on their way across the country, looking for a place to call home.

We took a look at their profiles. We had a phone conversation with them. They seemed like passionate, easy-going young people looking to learn as much as possible. We asked them what they were looking to gain, and discussed with them if we, as new farmers, would be able to fulfill their learning desires. Their reply: 'Everyone has something to teach!'

Our first impressions of Nancy and Andrew were spot-on. A seriously driven young couple, they asked great question after great question, explored every inch of the town while they were here, and were powerhouses while at the farm. No task was too menial or too challenging! They ripped stickers off of cardboard so we could mulch our paths, and they took scrap wood from our barn and built a fantastic chicken tractor in two days – something we'd been wanting to do but had neither time nor knowledge to accomplish.

We asked them if they would be willing to do it, and they completely tackled it. We passed along as much wisdom as we could and they accepted it gratefully. Nancy and Andrew had the opportunity to experience mid-west Wisconsin and get a feel for whether it was a place they may someday call home. Even though they were with us during the hottest days of the summer, what they brought to us was more than a pair of smiling faces and willing hands – they brought refreshment. Here were two passionate young people, taking what is given, asking for nothing, clearly glowing with promise and enthusiasm. So often it seems as though an individual's passion is ephemeral, too easily stopped by hitches and hindrances along the way. Theirs was not transient!

We hope we have inspired them as they have inspired us. Our first experience hosting Wwoofers has encouraged us to welcome other Wwoofers as our guests. Nancy and Andrew were right when they said everyone has something to teach – the opportunities are boundless! "

Emily provides a nice example of how the process of communicating with and selecting and working together with wwoofers works in practice. Of course each host's experience will vary, but this is fairly typical of what a conscientious host will encounter.

Patrice from Mana Kapu in Hawaii prefers applicants who express genuine interest in learning how to become a farmer. She expressed her enjoyment of the new energy Wwoofers bring regardless of their level of ability, so long as they have this sincere desire to learn.

In general hosts are looking for similar qualities in the volunteers: they hope the Wwoofers will be and feel involved; they enjoy sharing ideas; they thrive in the enthusiasm the new volunteers bring and show; they like (and usually expect) that they clean up after themselves; they appreciate open communication; and they expect work and living agreements to be kept.

Some hosts prefer volunteers who are new to

farming-blank slates- teachable students that they can share their knowledge with versus ones with experience; in contrast farms such as La'akea described above prefer the ones who bring a basic understanding and experience of permaculture and sustainability. In the end each host determines the level of experience they want or need, and in turn the volunteers choose the hosts that seem the best fit for them.

It is a process that at first may be awkward when it is unfamiliar, but gradually the more one hosts the process gets easier. Hosts learn to read between-the-lines and to decipher statements from prospective volunteer Wwoofers. There are of course no guarantees you will get the best, but then nothing in life is guaranteed, is it? Most hosts find that it is interesting to weed through the genuine requests to Wwoof, and learn to let go of the mass mailings that were sent without thought. They often wish they had room to host several more, especially when they come across so many interesting people.

Here are some examples from various hosts of the types of questions they use on their applications. New or present hosts can adapt them to suit their farm. Some are extensive such as this one from Sassafras Valley Farm in Missouri.

Sassafras Valley Farm Application

Contact information:

Full name

Current address

Rent or own

How long

Birth date

Phone number

Email address

Social Security number

Scan of current driver's license

Emergency contact:

Full name

Relationship

Phone number

Address

Email address

Previous work or volunteer experience:

Highest education level reached

Language/s spoken

Dietary issues and allergies

Physical limitations

Current Employer

Other organizations where applicant has volunteered and contact information
Description of training or experience that may be pertinent to the volunteer position desired.
Statement of and description of prior criminal convictions or offenses
References:
One or more personal references with contact information:
One or more professional or work-related references with supervisor's name and contact information:
Skills checklist :
Worked with animals? Which types?
Worked with hand tools?
Worked with power tools?
Worked with machinery or equipment?
Painting?
Landscaping?

Have you managed others?

Have you worked outdoors in the summer?

Worked independently

Reason for volunteering, what do you hope to gain from working here?

How did you hear about us?

Hours and days available for volunteer work?

How long of a stay are you hoping for?

Please initial each of these to verify that you have read them and agree to them:

1) Sassafras Valley Farm will expect a 2 week trial period with each volunteer

2) All volunteers thru WWOOOF or Workaways will be given a feedback on-line at the volunteer site.

3) There will be no use of drugs while on our property

4) There will be no firearms or weapons brought on to our property

5) Smoking of cigarettes will only be allowed outdoors

6) The local sheriff will be made aware of your being in our community and have a copy of this

application.

7) There will be zero tolerance for any infraction of the drugs and firearms rule

8) You will keep your guest quarters clean and the bathroom sanitary.

9) You will clean up after yourself in common areas.

Bill Greenleaf also generously shared several lists that he uses on Greenleaf Farm in Makawao, on Maui. They have been organic farming for several years, are very actively involved in the island's Farmers' Union, run a successful CSA with their vegetables and fruit, and they have hosted quite a number of Wwoofers so far. He has created many lists which help keep the farm well-organized, from supplies he suggests for Wwoofers to bring to the farm, to daily chores and routines, to the following procedures shown here:

Greenleaf Farm: General Rules and Expectations

Welcome to our Farm   -   Golden Rule Practiced

1. If needed, please ask for a set of sheets, pillow and blankets. Please wash and fold sheets and clean up completely after yourself at the end of your stay. Do not leave any of your belongings on farm w/o checking with hosts. We are happy to help you donate items no longer needed.

2. Please keep common areas picked up at all times. These include kitchen, closet, bathroom, outdoor sauna and shower areas. Towels should not be left at shower/sauna. You may leave shampoo and soap at outdoor shower. <u>Please use biodegradable products ONLY</u> as we have gray water recycling in showers and washing machine. Ask us about your products if you are not sure.

Do not leave dishes in kitchen sink. Clean up immediately so the area is clear for the next person. If you need to soak a pan, leave it in another area so others can use sink.

3. Please check in with hosts before using sauna. We can let you know if it's a good time.

4. There are many people living on the property. Please be respectful of them by keeping voices, TV and music low in early morning and after

9pm. Do not play music in studio so that you can hear it outside while working. Use your I Pod or ask for a small boom box.

5. You have agreed to work 25 hrs/week. The work day is Mon-Fri from 8-1. This amount of time allows us to take our time teaching as well as having a morning discussion before starting work.

6. Veggies and fruit can be picked for meals – check the list on the blackboard for what is available. Also check the Wwoof shelf in work area for extra from fallen fruit and harvesting. If you are not sure, please ask.

7. When working with another person please remember, talking is fine as long as you are both working at the **same time**. I Pod, MP3, etc. have a recent evolution history into the workplace. I would use one if I was doing a repetitive task that was boring. Farming does not fall into that category – it's more of a learning all the time. We request no ear bud music operation during farm time.

8. Put away all tools and clean up any area that you have been working on at the end of each job. Tools are very expensive to replace. Only use a tool for the job it is meant for. If not sure, ASK! Keep tool storage areas neat and remove personal belongings at the end of each shift. Please do NOT hang clothes or

any other items in trees - they are young and might have buds that could be knocked off.

9. If you leave an area for a short time where you are working with tools, make sure you put them down in a safe place where no one else can trip or otherwise get hurt by them.

10. Compost guidelines: We compost all vegetable/fruit waste. (Exceptions are - **rhubarb leaves (poisonous), avocado skins or pits - poisonous to chickens.)**

11. Chickens love weeds of all kinds except anything with thorns such as thistles and wild raspberry plants. They should be thrown away in dumpster. Collect and throw other greens into chicken yard any time. Also, please wash and save eggshells. They should be crushed and put in green dish in coop.

12. Whenever walking on property, if you see some weeds to pull, please do. Also, if you find any tools that another has left, please pick up and put away.

13. Look for rocks, especially after doing any kind of digging-collect and put in rock area (they mess up the mower blades).

14. If you see a job that needs to be done but don't have time to do it at that time-write it down on blackboard.

15. As a group, do a weekly clean-up in studio: clean kitchen, bathroom, vacuum and sweep, pick up personal belongings. Also sweep walkway outside front door, pick up plant debris around outdoor shower/sauna area and clean the sink. This needs to happen **EVERY** week. Pick a day with the group and let us know what day you have picked. We have a jar with all the jobs listed. Pass the jar around the group until they are all taken and keep these jobs for the week.

16. Familiarize yourself with recycling rules here. **EVERYTHING** that is recycled **must be rinsed** before putting in bins. We are serious recyclers and would appreciate if you would do the same while living here. When a bin is full, ask for guidance on how to separate recycling in our garage.

Regular trash is picked up early Mon and Thurs. Please put trash in brown dumpster on Sun and Wed eve if full.

17. If you want to have a fire, talk with Bill about the guidelines. No fires without permission any time. No fires during dry season.

18. Please keep your body clean. Showers should be taken at least daily on work days. Keep others in mind who might have to smell you and also keep in mind that we work with dirt and manure regularly and don't want it on the furniture, etc. If someone tells you that your BO is overwhelming-please honor them and shower. From November to March, short showers are necessary since the sun doesn't make as much hot water.

19. Have fun and take in the diversity of the environment on the island of Maui. The light is especially golden near dawn and sunset. The height of our trees makes this farm land a natural travel corridor for birds. See if you can notice the owl that hunts after sunset late into the twilight

20. Read prior Wwoof comments for ideas and please add yours at any time. If you've been to a great spot on the island, pass it on. Also feel free to share anything else about your experience.

21. If while using a tool it breaks in some way- please report it to us right away so we can fix or replace it before it becomes an emergency.

22. If you hitchhike home, please have the driver drop you a few houses before ours. Often people who pick you up want to be generous- others may want to see where you live, so for your safety and ours...

23. Quiet time outside around houses begins at 8pm. Please keep voices quiet and respectful. If you enter property after 8pm, please enter through upper gate.

24. Guest Policy: We recommend you do your socializing with people you meet on the island away from the farm. This is our home and we already have many people around.

If you meet someone who really wants a tour of the farm, please talk to us and we will set up a time for us or you to show them the land.

If you have a friend or family member visiting the island, we are happy to invite them for group dinner but please talk to us before making the invitation.

Bill's list is quite extensive, and should leave Wwoofers with full knowledge of his expectations, while leaving the door wide open for further communication if anything is still unclear.

I'm not including all of the other lists he generously shared, but one in particular was a *Waiver and Release of Liability, Indemnification, and Hold Harmless Agreement.* Several hosts indicated that they use forms such as this to provide some protection for themselves and their farm should anything beyond our control occurs. (Standard forms may be found on the internet that can be adapted for the needs of those who may consider this a good option for their farm.)

Naturally, once again, each farm host would tailor procedures according to their farm's requirements regarding any of these lists or forms and they are mentioned here to give food for thought in preparing your own lists and/or for your consideration.

The system works in connecting the two sides that compose this Wwoof adventure. Next we'll look into some insights on the actual day-to-day experience of how the interchange works with many commentaries from hosts. But first I'd like to mention some indications of what makes a good host in the eyes of prospective Wwoofers and to do this I am including in full the thoughtful remarks offered by Jonathan, the administrator of the WWOOF Hawaii Web site.

"We do not Host Wwoofers but we have learned a lot from visiting Hosts around the islands.

Many of the Hosts we have met are wonderful individuals with many talents and skills. We know it takes a lot to be a successful Host and can be a great challenge for many. It is very obvious to us when visiting a farm, which Hosts have overcome many of these challenges and which still struggle with them.

It is one thing to operate and run a successful farm, but it is another to run a farm and be a Host/Caretaker of many individuals who are constantly coming and going and many who know nothing about farming. A Host has to choose very carefully who they allow into their home and onto their land. Hosting one or two Wwoofers has its challenges but Hosting ten or more is a whole other ball game. Now you have to consider the dynamic of all of their personalities living together. Being a Host definitely presents many challenges, but when these things are managed well, it is a very rewarding experience for everyone involved.

A great Host leads by example while creating a space for everyone to grow and also become a leader. It is very important for the Hosts to teach the Wwoofers this way, for it is much more inspiring than them just being told what to do. When a farm becomes a dictator giving orders, the volunteers quickly lose a lot of their enthusiasm to help out and it creates a large separation between everyone. This usually spreads to a feeling of separation between everyone else and it is very apparent. When we visit a well-run farm, we know because we feel welcomed by everyone there. The Wwoofers have this excitement with life and what they are learning. They have been inspired and given the space to breathe and be themselves, and we know that they are happy and being supported where they are at.

A Host must also have a vision about what they are doing and why they are doing it. When the volunteers know what they are a part of and what they stand for, they feel very important and love making a difference. It is also important for them to be a part in creating the vision and how to get there. There is always room for improvement at a farm and those who are there can give the best advice on how to help it grow. A great Host will see this and will talk to their volunteers asking for their input on things."

Here also are some miscellaneous and anonymous comments that have been made by Wwoofers, gleaned from the pages of the Wwoof sites, just to give some examples of how they feel after their experience.

"We have learned so much from the Hosts we have visited and are very happy to see what they are doing. The love and care they have for the land and everyone else is very inspiring and we are happy to be part of such a wonderful program."

"We have never worked so hard in our lives! HA! .... Don't come here unless you are willing to WORK and work efficiently. For this particular community every hour is valued and accounted for: they have expectations of how long a task should take. With the skills and experience we brought with us, we were not always able to meet those expectations with our first effort and we needed guidance."

".... having a super time. The hosts are knowledgeable and friendly and more than happy to discuss their mission, farm dynamics, and market plans. I've worked at a number of different farms but this is the first time where I'm really getting specific knowledge on transplanting, growing

144

starts, and how they choose specific varieties for taste, etc. Can't say enough about the hosts, they're fantastic. Very much looking forward to the rest of my stay and coming again in the future."

"...although what I will remember the most are the kind people who live there. From the moment I walked in the door they took me in as one of their own. Every day ending with a delicious supper shared at the table with family."

Wwoofers naturally have their own ideals and expectations of what it will be like to volunteer on our farms. Some are perhaps naïve, perhaps going out on their own for the first time. So too we should realize we will be coming from different perspectives and the elements of experience, age, knowledge, hopes and ideals will all affect the decisions made on both sides.

While it seems judging by the huge number of positive remarks made by Wwoofers after their exchanges on the WWOOF web sites that the majority leave quite happy-and often eager to return or to try a new farm, naturally there are some who won't be wanting to Wwoof again , either there or elsewhere.

Sometimes they weren't cut to farm, or it may just be personality conflicts. Most often they didn't research enough or really know what they wanted to experience as opposed to what they were signing on for. Rarely, some will have legitimate complaints where a host did not provide as they should have or had promised and these hosts should be warned in the forums to other Wwoofers the same way as we share information about unreliable or dangerous Wwoofers.

Others complain that they feel overworked, even when they agreed to the set hours beforehand; were unhappy with the food, even when it was described as vegetarian, or 'junk-food free' beforehand; and still others have complained about the climate being too hot, or too muddy, or too wet, or too full of insects for their liking, even though those are natural conditions of farming.

These are not typical Wwoofer responses by all accounts of the many contributors here, or looking to the testaments online and in our collective guest books. We must be doing something right to have an overwhelmingly positive response overall! But anyone who has hosted a few dozen volunteers (or even less) will acknowledge that as hosts we must be prepared for the occasional non-match and just to accept their complaints as valid and recognize that the exchange is not meant to be.

In the next chapter we will look at advice from hosts who vary from being relative newbies to having hosted literally hundreds of Wwoofers over the years.

"The ultimate goal of farming is not the growing of crops, but the cultivation and perfection of human beings."

Masanobu Fukuoka

Chapter Five

Wwoofing Wisdom: Suggestions, Struggles &, Sharing Lessons Learned

So you have made your arrangements and are eagerly awaiting your first volunteer. You have, you think, a pretty good idea of what to expect. You will most likely go the airport, or train station, or bus station to pick up your helper. Personally, I love meeting the new Wwoofers and from what has been shared with me most hosts do. But to be realistic, even if your expectations are roughly correct the connection will probably still be full of little surprises, but these are what add to the exchange in immeasurable ways. Leaving yourself open to learning about new people of different ages and beliefs on a number of subjects, and coming from many different states and countries makes the Wwoof experience all the more interesting.

One of the statements I have been making ever since we started hosting five years ago is how much I enjoy having travelers come to us since we are not traveling nearly as much as we used to before we began farming. Having traveled extensively all of my life, it is a transition to have deeper roots and clipped wings. We are fortunate now to have an extremely capable caretaker for the farm when we do travel. Mark is not a Wwoofer, but has and does contribute greatly to our farm and homestead living on the land, enhancing our ever changing 'community', and enabling us occasionally to take some trips; but the adventures in other lands are still far less than before. For us, already having a deep, absolute love of unique cultures is also fortunate, and makes it all the more enjoyable to host people from diverse backgrounds.

Many hosts have written and shared similar views. For example, Lorraine from Moonrise Farms in Concho, Arizona said, "I can travel though their stories at a time in my life when I am rooted down and no longer wandering the world myself."

Likewise Carl and Lorna from Twin Brook Farms in Chealis, Washington say "With Wwoofers we can take a trip around the world without leaving the farm."

Some hosts do not have extensive travel in their past and enjoy the experience even more. Travelers from Europe and Asia or South America or Africa can offer new perspectives and enlarge our experiences, growing the community of the organic movement.

The social interaction is a huge part of the Wwoof exchanges. Of course we are focusing on our crops and growing the best food, but if we really think about it, the growing of human relationships is the greater result.

Holding hands across cultural divides.

Breaking down age barriers.

Sharing viewpoints and exposing ourselves to new ideas.

Seeing the similarities, rather than our differences, or despite our differences.

Knowing within how interconnected we are and how we are all part of the global community and how our actions affect one another.

I believe the Wwoof program does

a great service in fostering these human, one on one interactions. Hopefully the communication channels are open and the language barriers few. Hopefully most people who volunteer on our farms have this same idea of sharing socially and culturally as the hosts. We will each experience this aspect in our individual ways, but I can see from what many hosts say and from our own experiences here how important this is.

Not to say that hosts will not want their privacy. The depth of "communal" living will differ from farm to farm, and we each have our individual needs for personal space. But there will be time working together and during meal making and sharing meals together when genuine face-to-face conversations and honest sharing of ideas go a long way in uniting us and prove most rewarding in building new friendships.

This will not always work in practice; you may have more limited interactions, but I believe it is to be encouraged and is an integral part of what Wwoofing is. There is the agriculture side, and the culture side to sharing your home and farm with volunteers. The intention of Wwoofing after all is to be an educational exchange about both agriculture and culture.

We learn many things along with teaching the new volunteers about organic practices and sustainable living. Meredith from Red Fern Farm says "it is a balancing act," and I agree. There is teaching and learning. There is telling them your expectations and listening to theirs. We know most helpers, particularly the younger 20 somethings and even 30 somethings are looking not only to learn, but to have fun, and to travel and experience new places as well as meeting new ones via hosts and other Wwoofers.

We want people passionate about learning organic farming; they want a place to stay, sometimes more than to learn. Motivation varies. We need Wwoofers, who enjoy shared living, and we must enjoy it too or it won't work out well. Some farms have distinct separate living arrangements; some even to the extent that the Wwoofers prepare their own meals, so there is not very much interaction after the work day. Other farms share the cooking and cleaning and eat all meals together, and still others will have a mixed situation, maybe sharing dinners formally and leaving other meals to be more flexible.

Some of the farm hosts I spoke with have intergenerational households and the younger volunteers blend into this mix. In some cases the

Wwoofers will need to learn to interface with different age groups and diverse personalities as much as the hosts need to learn this. Not everyone has a past with shared living arrangements beyond the nuclear family, so this is again a social interaction learning experience beyond agriculture that is integral to Wwoofing.

The challenges of Wwoofing often revolve around communication and no one yet has been able to circumvent what sometimes results in expectations not being fulfilled. On the part of the host it is necessary to be very clear in our expectations, which may be similar, but will vary according to each farm.

Hosts state again and again that they explain the particular needs and amenities of their farms, but are astonished to find Wwoofers come with different expectations regardless. Most times the differences resolve themselves, but it is unfortunate that there be any difference, especially when we do extensive communication beforehand.

For example, we had a French Canadian once who came to us after working on a very large dairy farm, (we learned of this after his arrival)and in fact though he was quite young he was already planning to start a ranch of his own in the not so distant future specifically for raising dairy cows. He was very capable and mature and we have no doubt he will attain his goals. However, he was deeply disappointed that we could not make a gallon of milk available for him personally to drink on a daily basis, as he was used to this (and more in the way of dairy products) on the previous dairy farms that he had chosen specifically because they were dairy farms. What was astonishing to us is that he knew very well that we were growing cacao trees primarily, (and at that time strawberries), but had no farm animals at all.

He had expressed interest in sustainable living and learning to grow plants, and he especially seemed to like the idea of strawberries in March in Hawaii when he wrote, never mentioning anything about dairy once in his correspondence. We learned about those interests subsequently. We still don't see how we could have prevented the "disconnect" between his expectations and our stated reality.

Other examples contributed from various hosts have been similar where vegans offered to exchange on poultry farms and then left because they hated the realities of it, again not even stating they were opposed to eating meat. Others, who may turn out to be very good workers, and even remain friends with the hosts, nevertheless had some romantic notions that their time would be spent harvesting and eating fruit rather than weeding or mulching far more frequently, or expected that they would learn specific skills even where the hosts clearly did not have these skills to teach because they didn't raise that type of animal or grow those vines, or any number of anomalies.

In asking farm hosts to share some lessons learned along the way I heard many times about being patient, especially when teaching city kids about using tools and the most basic farm tasks. We need to be mindful just how new it is to them. And remember again and again that they are here to learn, rather than expect them to know things we know. Unless you are a farm that has specifically screened for experienced help, you will need extra patience and understanding. But you will be rewarded when you see them "get it", as every teacher experiences when their student has an "aha" moment.

One of the beauties of Wwoofing from the standpoint of the volunteers is that it provides an inexpensive way to travel. They are willing to work and are teachable in general, but not all will take it seriously, even if they stated at the outset that they were here to learn. Remind yourself now and then that not everyone is cut out for farming, or the rural life. To some it may sound like a glamorous adventure until they actually try it. You might find city slickers who can't handle the bugs, or the mud, or who had idea really just how dirty it could be.

This is one reason why some hosts choose to have short term helpers. They are usually quite enthusiastic to start and depart before they burn out. Some are so enthusiastic for the first couple of weeks and then the novelty wears off, and the work slows as well as the interest. Conversely, other farms don't like re-teaching the basics over and over again. They would rather teach new things as a progression with long term interns or apprentice type situations. But it depends again on the host and volunteer in each situation.

On this point I could not find consensus and hosts seem to be evenly spread along both opposing views, which of course are equally valid. It all depends on your personal outlook and needs. Those who prefer the short termers really enjoy the endpoint and see an accomplishment of a goal, and have enjoyed teaching to those who they feel are fresh and eager to learn. Those who lean toward long term stays-and even this varied from as little as a month to 6 months to be considered long term by the hosts- truly felt they received more valuable service from their helpers and that they were able to share much more with them from a teaching standpoint.

The exchanges of course need to be mutually beneficial. Wwoofers are able to learn about farming without investing in land or equipment, and without formally studying agriculture or trying things out at their own expense. In fact, there exist many formal, paid internships for the most serious students to study agriculture. Naturally they incur fees. Wwoof provides teaching that may often not be as in depth, but it certainly is a clear beginning for those who are considering a life of farming, without needing to go through the financial expense, by having the opportunity to exchange their sweat equity.

Hosts need help to run their small farm businesses, and/or to produce food for themselves. There is a give and take on both sides. Volunteers put in many hours of help without being paid, but they receive lodging and meals (or food to prepare) that they would otherwise have to pay for in addition to the teaching they receive.

Hosts already have paid for the infrastructure for the home or outbuildings where they accommodate the volunteers; sometimes these rooms were previously rented out and in those cases rent is forfeited in exchange for the help. In most cases hosts need and do purchase more food than is grown on the farm as well as other necessary supplies. (Although some farms can and do supply only what is grown on their own farm and volunteers need to buy extras.)

Often we take the time to cook healthy, nutritious meals, so Wwoofers do not have to cook after putting in their work day, which is another appreciated benefit. Some will have utility costs to factor in. So in the end it should and generally does balance out as a fair trade, albeit without money exchanged between the hosts and volunteers. These are varying individual arrangements that should be clear on both sides from the start. But is not free from either side-there is a value to all of these elements.

And whether it is a paid job or a voluntary exchange trade, honesty and fairness is and should be expected.

One of the principles that attracts Wwoofers is that they can step outside of the normal work and consumer-based economy to experience this direct relationship of growing their own food and enjoying it from "farm-to-table." After all is said and done, it is mostly about the food. Growing it, cooking it, preserving it, adding value to it by making new products for market, and of course the joy of eating it!

This brings up a multitude of opinions on what is good, healthy, nutritious food. And in my opinion and research I think it is impossible to have consensus. We may very well be in agreement about choosing organics because of not wanting chemical fertilizers, or herbicides, or pesticides interfering with our food chain or with the environment. But this is a rather different argument than what is good nutrition.

There may be many points where we agree, but more often there will be differences. Most likely the majority of Wwoof hosts will find young people who already have learned to avoid processed foods and preservatives. But you may find yourself educating others on why there is no junk food in your cupboards. We had one helper, a good worker with a great attitude, who during her two month stay had a couple of care packages of "junk food goodies" sent from her mom because she really had cravings for what she was used to, and we basically had none of these items around.

Just put a vegan vegetable famer and a grass-fed cattle rancher together and they will instantly have naturally arising and opposing views. If you haven't already experienced this you will come across countless variations in diet and what otherwise reasonable people disagree on as to what is the best food to eat. As we all know, reasonable people can and do still disagree on any given subject.

The gamut runs from the raw food enthusiasts, to vegans, to vegetarians ranging from lacto-ovo to merely lacto, or just ovo, to those who find fish acceptable, to those who eat poultry but not pork or beef, to those who prefer red meat and can eat it every meal.

Some will avoid sugar at all costs; some will grow sugarcane as a healthier alternative. Some feel taking honey from bees is wrong; others tap trees for maple syrup, or make birch syrup, or process agave cactus for the nectar. Some will be protein focused; others are content with the fruit and vegetable kingdoms. Some use dairy products with every meal, others avoid them completely. We read about new diet trends regularly, and about the contradictions that exist depending on whose statistics are used

But you can be sure that each one will insist that their diet is the best. (That is perhaps a discussion for another book, but definitely outside the parameters of this book.)

However, hosts do need to bear all this in mind before they agree to host someone. It is always best to be clear on what food you are willing to share, and cook, and allow in your homes and to what extent you will or won't adapt for helpers. You may be very willing to accommodate someone with food allergies and leave out certain foods from your cooking, but it is much more complicated to feed a meat eater if you are vegan and vice-versa. It can be done of course, but clear communication as always is a key component.

Neva, from Country Gardens Farm shared that initially she had some mixed feelings, as hosts often do. Because she had prior experience hosting foreign exchange students, she knew their maturity levels and expectations could vary wildly, and she had experienced a wide range of outcomes as most hosts do. She was one of several newly listed Wwoof hosts who was looking forward to their first exchange, and looking forward to the book and what they may glean from our collective ideas.

Other lessons learned passed on from hosts include the need for better screening in order to get the best fit between you and your volunteers. The overwhelming given advice is to have good communication. Several sent reminders to be flexible and to have back-up plans or tasks to be done on the farm. Often the weather can change in an instant, and without good planning the work day can be ruined, however, if you have a good plan B this can be avoided.

I heard often from hosts who loved cooking communally together with their woofers, and more often than that from others who preferred the consistency of one cook. But generally it seems hosts like having meals, or at least the evening meal, together with the volunteers. This is where the conversation flows freely and the social interaction thrives--- around the dinner table. Although some hosts still prefer that Wwoofers live and cook separately from the family and find the arrangement also works well.

The language differences you may experience if you are hosting volunteers from other countries usually should not be a problem. You should be able to determine from the letters, e mails, and phone calls beforehand about their ability to speak English; in every case you need to determine what level of language barrier you are able to effectively deal with on your farm.

We were personally surprised once when we had two young French boys come to Wwoof, and to discover that one was fairly fluent and the other basically knew no English. This made for more awkward flow of conversation since naturally the one boy had to translate all instruction etc. to the other. In hindsight it never occurred to us that only one would be able to communicate since they were traveling together, but we should not have assumed.

One person with both extensive farming experience and experience hosting Wwoofers is our neighbor, John Coverly, at Sweet Breeze Farm (formerly known as Kalapana Organics). John lovingly works at it literally from sun-up to sun-down. He was raised on a farm in Maine and has been farming organically in Hawaii for 36 years. Before there was Wwoofing here, he used to bring in people on his own to help him farm in exchange for teaching them, and today has several friends on the island that started farms after those experiences; so Woofing was the next logical step.

He is somewhat legendary among organic farmers on our island and known as "Ginger John" since he first started growing Organic yellow ginger in the mid-70s and exported it to the mainland. The local Japanese farming neighbors first gave it to him and taught him how it was used medicinally and how it was superior to the typical commercial white ginger.

Having had several farms he has a wealth of knowledge to share, especially about local crops since he has also has grown large amounts of native taro, and was instrumental in starting the practice of organic farmers of growing the very sweet, but non-acidic white pineapple, and recently he planted 1700 coconut trees on his previous farm.

John is very dedicated to the farming lifestyle, continually perfecting his own methods and following his personal philosophy, simply stated in his words, "Making life better each day I live by adding value to life in some way." He also acknowledges with clarity that "he feels fortunate, and accepts his 'life in the dirt' which is both rewarding and fulfilling as he is actively engaged in the mystery of creating food from seemingly nothing."

He genuinely enjoys sharing what he has learned with the Wwoofers and feels great when he knows he has helped them in any way. He is very proud when former helpers call or write or drop by, and is especially pleased to hear from those who continue onto other farms and then return to say his was the best Wwoofing exchange they had had and acknowledge that they learned very much. He has even converted a few into remaining vegetarians and smoke free.

His Wwoofers benefit from his very personal, deeply dedicated involvement with Korean Natural Farming methods learned from Dr. Cho and his associate, Dr. Park, here on our island, and which he has introduced into his farming methods over the last several years. John and his wife Jackie are integrally involved in the community with the "growing" of Natural Farming methods both of them sharing teachings about how farmers can utilize the indigenous micro-organisms in our natural environment that feed the soil and plants naturally.

While John still operates two farms and grows a wide variety of bananas, and ginger, turmeric, papayas, pineapple, and comfrey, among many other vegetable crops, the main crop these days is sugarcane. Jackie operates "The Sweet Cane Café in town, so the cane is grown and pressed primarily for the juice sold there, and through other commercial outlets. His farm is one of only two farms in the USA that is certified organic for sugarcane.

They also have dairy cows and the Wwoofers learn to care for the cows, and to make yogurt. They often have several helpers at a time, so it is a very lively interactive environment that their Wwoofers enjoy immensely from what I hear, and from having spoken to several of them.

Overall he likes the Wwoof program and is grateful for the many hands since he recognizes full well how much it takes to accomplish everything on the farm, and again, he really likes teaching. He admits however, that it is not always smooth and he often gets frustrated with the program.

No matter how well he screens he finds that in many instances volunteers don't quite match what they have stated about themselves during the phone interviews or in their emails. He makes an effort to discourage them from coming---because he wants to invite only those who truly want the farming life that he enjoys. He warns them that he is "old school" and that the work never ends for him, and he is told enthusiastically that they want this too and he gets hopeful; but it often quickly changes after arrival, and worse still he gets disappointed—as many hosts have experienced—when they leave long before their commitment time, in order to go surfing, or get a job, or something else unknown?

He sits down with on arrival and during their stays to repeatedly confirm that everyone has the same understanding about the work routines. He provides individual cabins, hot showers, laundry, and healthy vegetarian food, preparing two meals a day, and believes he offers the safe, comfortable, rustic, healthy environment that Wwoofers desire. And for the most part it works out well, particularly when there is good communication and when the Wwoofers arrive in good shape, ready to work and learn.

He doesn't ask for deposits, but is considering it because he has had to replace many tools due to carelessness and is at a loss on how to otherwise instill the importance of being responsible for tools. He tries to discern their emotional and mental stability beforehand, but does not find that very easy. He advises that there will be zero tobacco and alcohol on the farm; he tells them before arrival about the work hours and break times, wanting to prepare them as much as possible. Again we hear that sometimes it succeeds in bringing great Wwoofers, and other times it doesn't. For example, despite his clear warnings, they often are unhappy that they cannot smoke or drink.

Ultimately his love of farming and teaching,

and the frankly admitted need of helping hands wins out, and he does and will continue to persevere with Wwoofing and focus on the positive exchanges. Many return to do work exchanges again and again, so it obviously is working. For "Ginger John"---if he can instill a passion for growing good food in any of the Wwoofers, he knows his philosophy and organic lifestyle is succeeding.

Elena corresponded with me several times generously sharing her experiences as a host. She recognizes that she has learned a lot from other hosts and enjoys sharing her experiences in hopes of helping others. She said, "I have also gotten many great ideas from other farms as told to me by Wwoofers as to recipes, how they served meals, sleeping arrangements and farm practices." For example, she learned to start hand spreading some manure and mixing it with leaves and bark already by the side of the road to make a wonderful free road base as well as a great place to put those materials.

Their farm is Harmony Hill, a 3.5 acre ranch in the foothills of the Sierras outside Exeter, California near the entrance to Kings Canyon and Sequoia National Parks. They have Dressage horses, dairy goats, chickens and a variety of trees as well as herbs and berries. Additionally they have four seasonal grocery gardens and a major component of the farm is making a variety of goat cheeses. She begins by saying, " I never planned for our small family farm to become an international hub, but since January of 2008 we have hosted over 200 people from nineteen countries, and twenty six states, as young as 17 and up to age 70."

Elena says that she "spends a HUGE amount of time corresponding and making sure we are really a good fit. At present my main thrust is the horses and cheese making, so it is great when people come with those interests. We are not a commercial farm so I am not dependent on them. I almost always have more people wanting to come then I need...and I try to place the extras with my friends."

She was quick to add after our discussion of no shows and cancellations, "It is not for the faint of heart or really anyone who DEPENDS entirely on the help."

Lori Sands from Silver Wheel Farm in Pennsylvania operates her farm with her husband Ben; additionally they both currently work as teachers. Like many hosts Lori has done telephone interviews before, but it was sporadic. She plans on making it necessary in the future and more in depth and would like to have a farm visit beforehand as they will be trying for long term helpers rather than a large turnover. This would not be possible for all hosts, but again I have heard from others who also try for farm visits. In fact, despite wonderful experiences with their numerous Wwoofers over these years they are in the midst of rethinking their Wwoof program and have temporarily removed their profile from Wwoof USA for the time being.

Why? They are revamping their farm to change their crop mix and planting scheme in order to run it with less help. Another reason is that, "unfortunately, sometimes it was more trouble than the value of the work that got done correctly. Sometimes there are joyous surprises of wonderful people who fit right in and are no trouble at all. That is becoming rarer. IF we stay in the Wwoof program next year, we will definitely be doing telephone interviews beforehand."

She also recognizes that even with a phone call people are able to hide issues that will be apparent only after they arrive. Even with numerous emails where we think we are communicating well we find surprises. Another host shared an experience where they had exchanged no less than thirty three emails with one volunteer and yet when she arrived she lasted less than a day before leaving!

She added some of the little things that were not indicative of good helpers. For example they hosted volunteers who expected to use the car and others who announced in the middle of a task that they were hot and were going back to the house. One other issue was an increasingly high number of helpers with special dietary needs which proved expensive. I have had this comment (anonymously) from several hosts who had to consider the extra expense and the extra time to prepare different foods for the same meals.

Lori continued with this: "We have loved many of 'our kids', and they still come back to visit and help out on their way to their next adventure. Some kids come back every year. It is the newer ones who don't seem to 'get it', but I don't know what happened."

She wrote one more time after she pondered some situations she remembered.

"We have been lucky, and never had a criminal Wwoofer or one who stole from us, or used heavy drugs etc. They are generally respectful, ethical, intelligent people. Sometimes there are slackers who do not 'get' that they really have to do work. Some are rich kids on vacation. Some want to start farms of their own (our favorites!). Some are temporarily homeless. Some are chronic adventurers. Some are just plain 'lost souls'."

Lori continues with some very honest advice to Wwoofers. (Author's note: Wwoofers may or may not read this book, but regardless we can still hope they hear some of these thoughts). Many hosts share these same ideas, but most were less reluctant to state it, so I appreciate her pointing some of this out. If hosts feel alone in their experiences this will assure them they are not alone. I definitely understand her points even if I have not personally gone through the all of the exact same situations, as they do typify things that may occur. I hasten to add one more time strongly-these are not the majority of experiences which are largely very positive. We are hosts and most of us remain hosts despite the wrinkles because the benefits to all are huge and we love hosting. Nevertheless here is some of her advice.

"Read the farm profile and website thoroughly to avoid asking obvious questions when you arrive. We have dedicated "Wwoofer pages" on our website with an overview and a FAQ page. "

"The worst thing you can do is not show up. That is the only time I will go to the Wwoof USA site and trash you in the "Comments".

"I get many, many Wwoofer requests and I have to schedule and plan carefully to have the right balance all season. If you don't show up you have just screwed me."
"Do not judge the host's family, pets, house, housekeeping, friends, religion etc. etc. Wwoofers have openly criticized my messy Tupperware drawer, my use of a hybrid variety of beets, my choice of dinner music, and the fact that we use plastic bags. (Yes, we know they are evil, and we do wash and reuse them, much to the embarrassment of my children.) There are more, those are a small sample of the types of things rude people will say.
Keep   Your   Judgments   to   Yourself,   Please."

"Separation is essential in the Wwoofer/host symbiosis. That is why you sleep in the campers or tents, and we sleep in the house. My husband is an introvert and can't deal with all those kids in the house 24/7. Wwoofers have the run   of   our   house   from   7:00   am   -   Midnight."

"Do NOT clean out my refrigerator. The 'rotten stuff in a jar" was my 10 year old, precious sourdough starter that i was saving until bread-baking season arrived again. And it was given to me by a deceased friend."

"Do NOT do 'extra", or "surprise" weeding anywhere in the field or tunnels, because you just may eradicate 180 parsley plants that you thought were weeds. (Yes, this happened)."

Once again I have received several comments where hosts express their surprise about how the quality of the Wwoofers has seemed to decline and no one can quite put their finger on it. Some hosts have suggested that perhaps they are doing exchanges with those who are strictly out to travel and have an adventure and are not interested in farming at all, yet we/they couldn't discern that beforehand based on the request to Wwoof. Some volunteers seem not to distinguish Wwoofing with Couchsurfing unfortunately, and that is not a work exchange but merely a social one. Naturally, some volunteers are unsure of their futures and just trying things out which is quite understandable-as long as they have a good work ethic and come to the farms with a good attitude and willingness to work, as it is the basics of volunteering.

Back to Elena, who looks on these past several years hosting vast numbers of helpers as a wonderful experience. Here were her concluding comments.

"I thought of you this morning as I watched a Wwoofer raking mulch on a hill that will be green after the first rain because of her work, but she will not be here to see the results. I often have a pleasant afterglow of memory of a Wwoofer who did a certain job, started seedlings, turned over a garden plot, or built a raised bed. I think of that person warmly when I see the results of their work and often I write to them or send them a picture. *It is a wonderful thing to have this afterglow of ghost images of people who have been here and left a positive mark.*"

The Borner Farm Project hosts are still fairly new to the process, but Emily Betzler, the farm manager, generously added even more comments after their second experience with the following thoughtful outline of the lessons they have already learned.

"It was October. We'd lost one intern to college already and were about to lose the other. Garlic needed to be planted, a winter chicken coop needed to be constructed, and the last CSA boxes needed to be assembled. Our straits weren't exactly dire but they were getting there, so when a Wwoofer named Ian called us and asked if he could stop by in three days, it was a pleasant surprise! We knew very little about him save that he was coming from Wwoofing at another farm, and wanted to stay for a week at our farm before moving on to the Twin Cities. We took a chance and decided to host him. He got right to work upon arrival – it was pretty apparent that we'd made the right choice!

This was the second time we'd hosted a Wwoofer – we still didn't know much about what to expect. Here are four main things we learned during Ian's stay about the WWOOFing experience.

One is that it's important to make sure they know what you have to offer them in terms of knowledge and experience. Be sure to ask them what it is they've set out to learn on their adventure, and be honest about whether or not you can provide it. Unfortunately we didn't have our wits about us enough to interview him before he arrived but fortunately he was open to anything. An exit interview is also a very valuable tool – by the time they're ready to leave, Wwoofers seem more comfortable sharing their honest opinion of the farm, the hosts, and what might be done to improve experiences for future Wwoofers. Right before he left us, Ian helped us plan out a more structured approach to selecting and hosting Wwoofers.

Lesson two is that some Wwoofers are looking for more than just experience in the farm field; some want to gain experience in all aspects of a place. Ian jumped right into the community by coming with us to our weekly knitting night and gamely picking up a pair of needles. He hung out with us during a movie night. He went with our intern to another farm to help milk cows, and he even stayed an extra day to help us prepare for, and to attend, a harvest potluck. He met many new people and learned skills he wouldn't have had he wanted to use his evenings in other ways. During the exit interview he explained how much more valuable his experience with us had been because of his interactions with the rest of the community.

Lesson three was a reminder that WWOOFing is a two-way street. Ian, though still a beginner with most things farm-related, had spent the summer biking from farm to farm and picking up lots of knowledge. He had seen many ways of doing many things, whereas we knew of only our way of doing things. He offered helpful suggestions on ways to be more efficient in the field and brainstormed ideas for the construction of our chicken coop. We invite people to stay at our farm in order for them to learn from us, but we must remember that everyone has something to teach: a good host will ask the Wwoofer what they think and be open to any suggestions.

The final lesson from Ian's stay with us is that open and honest (and frequent) communication is key to a fun, successful experience for both Wwoofer and host. Making sure both parties know what they want from the other as soon as possible is vital. With this advice under our belts we're looking forward to many more great Wwoofers passing through!"

Eric from Cold Creek Ranch located in Clifton, Arizona shares a custom with my husband and me in the screening process. We agree on discouraging applicants and then taking the ones who are insistent. We find that when we point out the hard work and the fact they will be seeing the deep blue sea while they work, but only having the option of going there after the work is done, they often change their minds.

It may sound counterintuitive, but we feel this is best for everyone. Sometimes the idea sounds exciting or glamorous (!) until they come and realize it is hard work. In this way neither side will be disappointed after an arrival and have to change plans at the last minute. The ones who persist have a clearer view and truly are eager to learn and don't mind the work.

Carolina from Ka Ulu o Kalani, on the Big Island of Hawaii (whose name means heavenly abundance) feels the need to stress before arrival that the work is physical. She advises that prospective Wwoofers should know that they need to have stamina and endurance; they need to be physically fit, and they need to have a good attitude and be conscientious workers. Some of this may seem to go without saying, but perhaps this is good advice to let your volunteers know before hand, or if you use an application to have as part of your questionnaire for information. Carolina feels that those who start off this way also leave healthy and happy.

A minor point that comes up infrequently is that in general hosts do not find it easy to have volunteers with very young children. Naturally, this seems opposed to being in a wonderful environment in a rural place of beauty that should be a natural place to have children. However, the point that came up was that it is not easy to work and watch small kids and keep them safe at the same time, so specific arrangements have to be made. I did not hear from hosts who provided an easy solution, but I imagine farms are accomplishing this. Surely with imagination and perhaps staggered hours, something satisfactory can be worked out. Having said that I also had correspondence with hosts who brought in entire families to live and Wwoof, showing once again how all will depend on your personal situation.

Dawn from Goodness Grows in Bedford, Pennsylvania reminded me that "farming is not for everyone". Sometimes when it is apparent to you as a host you will find yourself in this awkward position. She advises just taking then aside and having a frank discussion and asking them to leave.

Meredith from Red Fern Farm in Gray Court, South Carolina has several management tips to share which are included here together with miscellaneous suggestions from others. She suggests that to start ...

"You should always give clear instructions and work alongside your volunteers, especially in the beginning. You will learn when they can work independently-but it may take a few tries! Teaching them to ask questions is wise; sometimes they hesitate and don't want to trouble you, but you are better off explaining that it would be more trouble if they don't ask and instead do a job incorrectly, creating new work to correct the problem.

Give them an overview of what you expect but then give them some space rather than looking over their shoulder to criticize. In the end you will usually be pleasantly surprised and everyone will be happy. Learn to delegate and remind yourself that you are there to teach and help. It is hard for many of us to let go of the control, but learning to trust and relax can be very beneficial.

There needs to be a balance between trust and your own standards of quality control. This will naturally vary more if you have marketable products versus personal food production. If you give good guidance and instruction you are more likely to get good results. If you have tried all this and it fails, then perhaps you must revert to previous advice to take them aside and ask them to make other arrangements elsewhere."

You may be lucky in that they have had good training at previous farms. We find we have quite a few first timers and often volunteers who only do this once; not because they don't enjoy it , but rather it was just something they wanted to experience before moving on to their other non-farming careers.

Again we hear the repeated mantra to be patient-as all teachers must. Beyond patience most often hosts suggest a lighthearted attitude. Not always easy if you have deadlines and CSA customers to deliver to or markets to supply, but a big part of sustainable living is not to fall under the old principles of economic needs taking the forefront and the good food becoming secondary.

Diane from Joe's Nuts, a farm in Captain Cook, Hawaii shares her insights and what she has learned. She recognizes that each person has his or her own unique personality, and different sets of values and experiences, and their own personal issues, and that as hosts we need to work with those personalities. She believes in being firm and accepting the differences. Occasionally someone has to be asked to leave, but it can be done with dignity and style. She believes that most Wwoofers are good and by keeping it simple, smart, and happy it works, and she finds the interactions fun and interesting.

She also has noticed that for their farm a period of about four to six weeks works best, because she observes a turning point of volunteers feeling too comfortable after this. Other hosts still prefer shorter and or longer terms if exchanges, so each host will find what works best for them once more.

The struggle for one host with longer periods of Wwoofing is that it becomes "too long" if everyone isn't clicking, yet if it is "too short" she didn't feel able to train them enough to be independent workers. In her case, she is looking for a long-term intern who will be dedicated to learning and become more of an employee. She enjoyed the Wwoof experiences, but felt the limitations too much for their situation

At Joe's Nuts they give Wwoofers their own space away from the house, which is preferred by some hosts, yet not always possible depending on the accommodations you have to offer. (Other hosts simply prefer them to be living in the house as a family.) Diane also believes in teaching them to be independent and to simplify. She teaches them to hitchhike, and I admit I do the same, since I have done it much myself in my past and still see it as very safe on our island. (I still give lifts to hitch hikers too.) This may not be an option in most places on the mainland.

Candice from Urbiculture Community Farms in Denver, Colorado summed up their relationship with Wwoofers:

"Farming is hard work! Our multi-plot farm

has fourteen plots to maintain, a CSA, donations to shelters, a farm stand on one of the sites, a school garden which incorporates a youth program and a youth run farm stand, fruit trees throughout the city that we harvest, and lots of wonderful volunteers to coordinate. That being said, we rely heavily on our Wwoofers to help us throughout the season. We require a two month or longer stay because we want to educate our Wwoofers about urban farming in hopes that they become farmers.

This is our second year and we are grateful to those that have come along on their journeys and have put their love, sweat, tears, laughter and gratitude into this beautiful project we have going on in Denver. But there are some that think that farming and urban agriculture is this fantasy world, where they will be doing good, but do not realize how much work it is. And so we have had some that have come and gone quickly, but we hope that they too will bring a wholeness with them along the rest of their path. It is work, but it is humbling work that is creating a better world."

Genie from Spencer Creek Grange near Eugene, Oregon contributes some ideas of what makes it work in their experience. They view their Wwoofers as having been friendly, polite, and respectful and recognize that they even anticipated the needs on the farm, which was wonderful. In turn they reciprocate with respect, and politeness in a friendly atmosphere, and added occasional treats of pizza and ice cream, even though normal fare is to eat "off the land". While that is happily consumed, the treats always are appreciated; we too know the value of this as do many hosts.

She adds that having a positive attitude yourself is essential, as is continuously putting yourself in the other's shoes and to see the best in them. She advises always remembering the Golden Rule. In closing she said, "So much of our life has improved since they came along."

Gratitude and showing your appreciation for the woofers goes far, and undoubtedly the response is volunteers reciprocating with a great attitude. Sometimes we need to be grateful and express it, even when the results aren't what we hoped for. It seems to go without saying, but perhaps making gratitude a priority is a good thing. Sometimes they make you feel overwhelmed with gratitude.

You can still apply standards and discipline but by having a lighter attitude the work generally goes better. This applies to doing your best to treat Wwoofers well and getting good work in return. It will not work 100% of the time perhaps, but most often it does. "

We like to take Wwoofers on little excursions around our island to see the volcano, or some of the waterfalls, or go to the beach on days off. We are lucky to have a waterfall and natural swimming pond a short hike from our cacao grove, so Wwoofers can have a great time right here---depending on the rain! We don't make the little excursions as often as we like, usually because there is more work to be done here even if they have the day off. (Case in point-my husband works much longer hours and days than we ask of the volunteers.) But it is always enjoyable, and we feel a good part of the personal interactions that we like very much comes from sharing these events.

The light attitude, the laughter, going off on little adventures for the fun of it, cooking together --- all of these add to the social experience and foster lifelong friendships.

We personally have had several Wwoofers bring their parents to visit our farm, (and yes, they did ask first) both while they were Wwoofing and in other cases after they completed their stay with us, and we always enjoyed this. Others have brought friends by with permission on some non-working days. Sometimes we have enough social interaction here already, especially when we have had four helpers at a time staying on the farm. Other times there are not enough young people around so we don't mind friends coming by when they are not working. On occasion we have had gatherings on our farms inviting Wwoofers from other farms. For us this was a great time. There are farms that are able to do this on a weekly basis, sometimes where farms share work and do many activities in tandem which is great community interaction.

Things change, situations vary-every farm will have their own way of creating the right atmosphere for a thriving farm, happy helpers, and a good experience for all.

"Even if you have a lot of work to do, if you think of it as wonderful, and if you feel it as wonderful, it will transform into the energy of joy and fire, instead of becoming a burden."

T.T.Rimpoche

Chapter Six

The Joys of Wwoof Hosting

Over the few years we have been hosting Wwoofers, some of our non-farming friends have wondered aloud about why anyone would come and work for free on a farm. In spite of appreciating our lifestyle and our beautiful surroundings, the work aspect was a puzzle-until we expressed the many wonderful benefits of these exchanges. We view it as a win-win situation for hosts and Wwoofers, and the overwhelming majority of responses I received when inquiring of many other farms was this same very positive view.

More than one host described the experience as akin to the 'back to land' movement of the 60s and 70s. One said, "It is the baby or brainchild of the openness and trust of that generation."

Personally my husband and I each happily experienced living on farm communes during the early 70s and can see that relationship. Gene and Vicki Doyle , who own and operate the Last Word Ranch in Cerrillos, New Mexico have some related ideas since Gene compares it to hitchhiking-another activity that was ubiquitous in the 60s and 70s. Gene wrote, "We have only been involved with Wwoofing for a short while now. Like you, we are very committed to helping it to succeed. and also like you, there have been some 'wrinkles'. We could avoid many of those wrinkles by being more selective and doing a more thorough job of interviewing the candidates before we bring them in but we do not want to get too formal with the process either."

Despite his mention of the wrinkles, I found their statements to be best included here speaking about the beneficial joys of hosting. What he said resonates personally with me, (I have done my share of hitchhiking back in the 70s) and I have included it in its entirety.

He describes the relationship of hosts and Wwoofers this way. "Their paths and ours need to intersect for as little or as long as they are meant to. For us it is more like hitchhiking than a business arrangement, or a job interview. I guess one would like to pick the type of person that you give a ride to, or get a ride from, but the varied experience of just letting it happen as it will, makes the journey a lot more interesting. And like hitchhiking, you start out with a select pool of participants. Those who would give you a ride are more than likely generous and well meaning. Those who are hitching a ride, (it has been my experience anyway), are adventurous and interesting, heading places with determination and sometimes the only way that they can. Some are just desperate to get down the road, but you do not usually find Wwoofers like that, at least we have not.

As with the Wwoofers, you have only a brief glimpse of who the hitchhiker is. You judge them on how a hitchhiker stands, how they dress, what their situation might be before you pick them up and you make a quick decision and it works out, or it does not, but nothing great has been lost and something worthwhile has transpired, they got a ride and one has shared some company outside the norm of everyday life.

The Wwoofers do not seem to be much different. They are for the most part heading somewhere with determination and are adventurous (they are going to, often times, remote areas on little more than a two paragraph summary of what they are getting into and they are willing to take on the risks and possible disappointments with few reservations). So too we take them in based on only a couple of paragraphs of "Can I come and stay with you for a while"? In the very worst of the situations it has cost us a few meals and some patience lost, but for the most part the relationships have been mutually beneficial and for our part, we feel we have helped someone along the way with good example, some lessons in sustainability and a memory they can keep along their journey to wherever they are going to."

Eric Schwennesen from Cold Creek Ranch in Clifton, Arizona has also stated his experiences very well. "In the end we have seen a whole aspect of world existence that couldn't be had any other way; we trade our knowledge for their enthusiasm and we both come away from the experience better for it. Wwoofing offers an essential look into the world which is different to manage any other way."

His place is a 10,000 acre cattle ranch that raises and direct markets naturally grass-fed-or in his words again-"cactus-fed" beef. He has hosted more than 80 Wwoofers from ages 17 to 71 over the last thirteen years and has had several return more than once. I liked hearing that five former helpers have gone on to study veterinary medicine-showing how the benefits extend far into the future. Eric's experience has been mostly delightful "with an occasional dud for contrast". He found the Wwoofers to be upbeat, positive, and eager to learn. Like many of us he notes how they leave photos and good memories behind, and an occasional scar (usually on a tool or piece of equipment or machinery).

Sam Lorch from Sambo Berries shared his hosting experiences, focusing on the positive. Most hosts responded this way and we have the same attitude-when less than desirable situations arise, it is maddening, but it is best to let go, learn and move on.

In his words- here is Sam's thoughtful commentary.

"The WWOOF Organization was founded on sound principles and ideas, and for my part, has been an exciting interaction of people who, for the most part, have little (if any) farming experience. Most of them have the desire to learn, and that's good enough. The ones truly interested in learning about sustainable farming, or farming for a living, are the ones I enjoy hosting the most. Some come in very good physical condition and love the outdoor work, while others just want to 'know how'. Either way, any knowledge and experience we can give them on their road to 'feeding themselves and hopefully others' has to be beneficial to them at some point in their life.

As a host, I must be concerned with a fair amount of labor in return for hosting accommodations, food, etc. but I try to keep my focus on teaching them and getting them necessary experience from the tasks I ask them to accomplish. Most of them will not end up growing the crops I do, and may not live in a tropical environment, but the diversity of gardening knowledge they accumulate along the way will give them the basis to get started, and as all gardeners know, growing food is not always easy and one will need to adapt his/her knowledge to the particular plants they grow and their location and weather conditions.

I believe the best we can hope for is to motivate the Wwoofers to TRY, and once they begin to garden on their own hopefully many of their experiences and things they have learned will come back from memory and they will begin to adapt and succeed. If they never are able to grow their own food, at least they leave here with an education about the food they are eating---from grocery stores, etc., and so they begin to be more careful about their diet----reading labels and questioning some ingredients and additives, and in general, just plain eating better food. This also must be considered a positive thing, for it will take much more than just us 'farmers' to change the way the world is fed."

Green Rob from Sun One Organic Farm in Bethlehem, Connecticut has hosted about sixty Wwoofers to date and reminds us that Wwoofers are often an integral part of the operation. This may not be true for all farms, but many rely on the system as part of the design of how their farm runs. He has had fantastic results with the helpers and has been able to hire on a farm manager and assistant from former Wwoofers.

And Lorraine from Moonrise Farms in Concho, Arizona points out that "many leave with an experience they won't soon forget and everyone leaves their mark on the farm in return."

Sonja from Apple Pond Farm in New York

shared pleasant memories of her Wwoofers. She wrote, "Our experience with WOOF. has been positive - from outstanding to very good. For us, it is a chance to make new friends - especially those from Europe (our favorites right now). A couple have come back for another, even longer stay. I visited one in the south of France. In our set up, they live with us, share meals - both eating and cooking - and that is great. I usually have to remind them not to work so hard! Though only a few have farm skills they have all been motivated to pitch in - great for us.

We have done our best to make them welcome, take them places etc. be generous. There are reminders here for WOOF -the gate to the garden built by Samuel/ France, the crazy beautifully painted walls in our chicken house (two women from California, the doors to the barn grain room/Isabel of France, the great mulching job that Mallory did/USA, the onion tart I made compliments of Francois Xavier a French dairy farmer....we have named our Il De France ram FX after him, too!"

Personally, I know I can't look at the strawberries without remembering all the hard work from Ivy and Lucy, and every time a day lily blooms I see Travis. My favorite "IQ" lamp that was finally put together thanks to architect TJ, and once again by Grant when we moved it. We will be ever reminded of Ben and Grant when we park the car since they did quite a bit of hard work stacking lava rock for the rock wall. The garden gate says Trent each time it opens and the cacao trees are indelibly marked by all of the Wwoofers who have passed through! Beyond the reminders on the farm and plants they have left little bits of themselves with drawings and jewelry they made and gifted, and in recipes we shared, and in foods we especially enjoyed with one another.

One very talented musician, Michael from Colorado, taught himself to play the ukulele while here for just a few weeks and wrote a thank you song for us and our farm that made us cry. Ivy from Wisconsin made us a lovely and treasured video memory when we were still in the very beginning stages of the farm which years later new Wwoofers enjoy. Chris handcrafted a hunting bow from our bamboo. There has been music-making from some very talented kids, and storytelling and travel tales; some bring and share yoga lessons and computer skills and teach us new things about the latest in technology (e.g. this is how we discovered Pandora), and others have shared their personal knowledge of herbs and other alternative healing insights. We've played games and cards and scrabble, watched movies and talked for hours on end. It has all been memorable and we want to continue creating those memories. Once again, thoughts similar to these were shared from several farm hosts.

We are old enough to call almost all of them "kids" and most feel like our kids while they are here and we hate seeing them leave. They fill the place with laughter, and enthusiasm, and an open fun attitude. They fill our homes and farms with uplifting energy. We 've had some who were quiet and kept to themselves, but the majority have been interactive in the best way while we each treated the other side with respect and the all-important personal space.

Tina spoke to me from the Walking J Ranch in Arizona. A key element to their ranch is their poly-culture farming incorporating a wide variety of animals, rotational cropping and grazing, using the animal manures naturally for their crops and developing healthy soil with probiotic, beneficial bacteria.

When we discussed the Wwoof hosting she mentioned how initially they were caught up in the enthusiasm of the program and let anyone come who asked, but they had learned to be more discriminating going into the middle of their second year. Now they use reference checks, do phone interviews, and in general try to weed out those who won't be a good fit beforehand. They even will send out a contract to prospective Wwoofers outlining what they will teach and what they can learn on the ranch.

They also realized how much they value their family privacy and have built separate comfortable quarters for the Wwoofers and established some boundaries. They provide food and a stipend to cover items they are not able to provide from the farm. She says the arrangements work out great for them and together with the pre-screening they are very pleased with the program. They always try to be aware if any conditions need changing as they go on.

Other farmers have shared that they shed tears when their helpers leave and hope to host for as long as they are farming because they enjoy it so much. Scott Brodie from Red House Farm in Boulder, Utah says he knows he couldn't do it without them and in fact it may be the most important aspect of his farm.

Farmers with children of their own feel that not only have their lives been enriched, but their kids benefit from the friendships with the Wwoofers. Over and over hosts report how they stay in touch with former volunteers and as we say-have made lifelong friends. Most hosts recommend the program to other farms that were unfamiliar with it and continue this practice.

It is a wonderful way to continue cultural exchange –especially as I mentioned previously from my own experience and from many other hosts, especially when you miss traveling. Here is what John from Forever Yong Farm in Arizona stated so well. "Since we love to travel but can't leave because we are 'down on the farm' we can travel vicariously through the Wwoofers and their stories. The world now comes to us..."

That strikes a chord with many of us.

They come from all walks of life and sometimes from other countries and cultures, so we cannot help but find it interesting. You will find teachers and nurses and firefighters and others from diverse situations who come to learn about our world and who can teach us about theirs. The learning flows in both directions.

And of course they appreciate good food from the garden, from the fresh vegetables that they participate in growing to the fruit from the orchards, to the healthy, lovingly prepared nutritious meals (and desserts!).

Where there is good communication and an atmosphere of flexibility the good far outweighs the bad. There will occasional duds and mishaps but we need to keep it all in perspective. Keeping gratitude in the forefront and letting them know we are grateful is important for all.

One female host says "We all have our strengths and I love learning about the volunteers' diversities, and of their lives, experiences, and skills."

She especially enjoys teaching people things for the first time and recognizes that while she has been sometimes amazed at the lack of knowledge in new Woofers about even simple garden tools, she remembers that she is completely in the dark about urban public transportation, for example, and so she keeps it in perspective.

Elena from Harmony Hill talks about some of her initial exchanges. "Our first visitor Daniel, had just graduated from a prestigious University summa cum laude and wanted to get his hands in the dirt before entering graduate school. We hosted a young French girl who hitchhiked across Canada. We have had professional people and lost souls but all have added something, in their own way, with love, to our farm from murals, to gardens, to taking care of the animals. I have learned something valuable from each visitor and am eager to meet whoever travels our way.

Most have become family. We were hosted by our former visitors when we visited Europe this summer and a wonder young French Canadian woman managed the farm beautifully with the help of some other wonderful and loyal Wwoofers. We could not have paid people to take better care of our property and animals with the little details only a friend or family member would know to keep everyone comfortable and happy including taking a shower with our Parrot. Not every visitor has been perfect; a few have been energy draining disasters; but the overwhelming majority have improved our life and farm and overall happiness as we continue to expand our little motion normal community."

Later correspondence brought additional interesting remarks. Many people have told her that they were experienced horsemen or women, but actually only five or six, a small percentage could ride. Many have said they could cook, and liked to cook, but again she found that to be true for only a small percentage of the time. So in her words, "It is important to keep a sense of humor, embrace the unexpected, be flexible and most important not truly depend on the stated skill or even arrival. Always have a backup plan."

She continues, "The flip side of this is I have had many people who did not mention a skill that turned out to be awesome. I have had artists leave unique marks and learned to cook some fabulous things I never could have imagined. Almost everyone has something beautiful to leave on the farm, and to enrich our lives and those of other Wwoofers."

Jeanmarie from Second Chances in Mena, Arkansas (an LBGT friendly farm) has this to share about why she is part of WWOOF. "As I get older (near 68) I think about grooming potential successors for my projects. I have a compulsion to preserve my hard won skill set and knowledge by gifting it to these young folk with the desire and aptitude to learn. Wwoofing becomes a synergistic event that is truly a win/win for all involved."

When the hosts too have a willingness, such as Jeanmarie, or Sam to teach, and the helpers have a desire to help and learn, then in most situations it doesn't take too much more to have things go smoothly.

Sara from Elk Creek Gardens in the Cascade Mountains in Oregon believes she has had an approximate 80% success rate from forty-six Wwoof exchanges as far as getting some help that worked out well for living and working with for two weeks to three months at a time. She took the mentoring seriously and she also tried to point each Woofer towards the information that each seemed to be seeking. She knows that some of the helpers, "just wanted to skim the surface of farming, having come to the farm rather than go home that summer" and that many of them had a romantic notion of living on a farm, but she also found that none of the them had the necessary stamina required to take on farming individually.

She added that she "found some who were passionate about the politics and the methods of organic food production, and hounded me for as many questions answered as they could get out of me in the time we had together. I always learned something from each one and I never had any take serious advantage of me."

Amy from The Small Family Farm in Idaho states her feelings quite well when she says, "One of the things I am most grateful for is the influx of interesting people young and old who have passed through this small town and small family and exposed our son to new ideas and ways of life. The experience is invaluable and has left our son with a broadened perspective on life and its possibilities." She of course felt closer to some more than others, but felt that "All of them have been respectful, and have contributed their fair share of work, and been interesting company."

She continues, " I really like how in this day and age full of trouble and a strong-arm-of the-law mentality, we have been able to welcome people in our home and family, share ideas, and thoughts, and request work with integrity. It's never about money (a rare concept in the modern world), it is just about having people help to meet each other's needs in a trusting environment. And we haven't been taken advantage of once."

She also expressed using her intuition with her good judge of character, and when she has had an 'iffy' feeling she just doesn't even invite that person. I agree with this and her concluding remark: "But nothing is foolproof, and we have just been lucky."

Another anonymous comment says the folks they have hosted have been dedicated and hardworking, with very little, if any, trouble at all. He adds, "Being a part of WWOOF has made things

206

work better here for me, and the future looks even brighter." He is turning away Wwoofers because he can't accommodate all the requests he gets.

Linda owns and operates McDonald Ranch which is unique and where as she explains, "We 'raise children' instead of crops." They try to teach the children the values of organic life styles and actually do qualify as organic with the goats they raise for milk production. They have found WWOOF to be a very interesting and helpful resource and realize it will be especially helpful as they grow older and less physically capable in their senior years. McDonald Ranch has had hundreds of visitors over the last five years. They find that the helpers have brought experience and information they could not have had otherwise. "There have been many who have left who built things on our ranch that has made our work so much easier and/or more efficient for years after they leave. Others have left recipes, memories and, of course, friendships we will always treasure."

Linda added, "Something else that is interesting to me is to be so much older than most of the guests who come through. What I find interesting is passing on our 'old fashioned ways and values'. While it may not be appreciated by some, it seems to be at least respected by most. And, of course, the young adults help so much in keeping us more current with today's affairs and technology.

Jerome, on a neighboring farm on our island has said he has more requests than he can possibly handle and is ever grateful. He attributes this partly to a You Tube video that some former Wwoofer made of his farm that applicants often refer to.

Genie at Spencer Creek Grange in Oregon finds her Wwoofers being good ambassadors for the program as they help her at the Farmers' Market. Now neighbor farms are asking her how they can get involved and even how to start their own farms. The organic movement is evidently growing! But the personal benefit is even better for her. "My daughter adores them", she says, "and they will be very much missed by the whole family."

Revelyn Rawdin and Patrick Morris speaking about their farm which is temporarily leased to others, simply stated that from their perspective regarding hosting Wwoofers "We loved it!" But they recognized that they were also "exceptionally" lucky to get two young people who really were willing to learn about farming from the ground up.

At the time they were hosts they also held full-time jobs while they farmed, so in their situation they needed people who could really manage on their own. Revelyn said, "Both Pat and Molly were willing to dive right in and worked every bit as hard as we do, which in our case was critical to succeed. In return we tried to take them hiking and to see the sights and beauty of our area.

I think that the realization that I've come to is that life is a bell curve and that at this stage of our lives (we've passed the hump and we're on our way down the other side) it's time to mentor those that are coming up, trying to find their way in the world and learn the skills that we were eager to learn at their age. And so we are Wwoof hosts - not because we need to farm (although we do) not because we cannot hire the help (in fact we cannot), but because it provides an opportunity to mentor those that are willing to share themselves in order to learn and we in turn share ourselves and what we have in order to help them."

She did add some caveats that she wishes could be enforced perhaps through the Web site. Like many hosts she got many exceedingly vague, uninformative requests simply stating, "I want to work on your farm."

As a host I couldn't agree more with the frustration this brings and have myself advised some who queried that they simply didn't provide anything for us to go on to determine if we should invite an exchange. The Wwoof sites clearly tell helpers to post a profile, but quite a large number do not, and then do not offer anything with their requests either. I have heard wwoofers lament that not all hosts responded to them, but usually this is the reason.

We implore the potential Wwoofers to complete a profile and provide a personal letter to each farm they are interested in if they truly want a good response. There are also a large number of Wwoofers who write beautifully detailed letters and fill out applications thoroughly, so it is in fact the other Wwoofers who are competing for the spaces and will likely get them because they have supplied sufficient information.

In fact here are a few humorous, uninformative, and generally unappealing requests from my own files:

Hey man My name is xxxxx I am 21 and am interested in your farm. I am new to woofing so if you could just get back to me with some questions for me I would appreciate it. Thanx .

Polite –yes-but …the next one is amusing but still lacks substance.

… Hey y'all, my name is xxxxx and I am itching for a new experience. Your farm sounds amazing and I would love to be considered for the open position. If the position is still open, hit me back. Cant wait to hear from you and hear a little more about y'all.

Hi, this is xxxxx. I wonder if you need any WWOOFer during Dec 15 till Jun 14. If you do, please email me.

Hello my name is xxxxx and im interested in your farm! please email me back with more info on the process

And finally this one that just came in while

I was writing:

hello, was looking to work for you in the near future,
thank you, xxxxx

I know from talking and writing to many hosts that most of us get some of these, and again we respond much better to informative requests, so we hope prospective volunteers will write good introductory letters.

Now to share some more sentiments of great interactions here is an essay written by Rhio, a host from Rhio's Gardens, which again was so detailed I chose not to compile it with other comments. (More of her thoughts appear in the chapter on "wrinkles.")

Wonderful and Wacky Wwoofers by Rhio

"We have been hosting Wwoofers for approximately seven years on our 'truganic',

Biodynamic farm in the Catskill Mountains of New York. I have rarely had a negative experience with my Wwoofer helpers.

One time I had a volunteer from Japan. He stayed for approximately two months, and toward the end of that time, it started to snow lightly. At the time, he was digging many two foot holes for some fence posts to enclose a second large vegetable garden. We told him that he didn't have to work in the snow, but he said that he had never experienced snow before. He was happy as a lark out in the garden, and refused to come in. His joy and enthusiasm was truly delightful. But, occasionally, we insisted that he come in for a hot cup of tea.

Another time I had two couples from Canada take their annual vacation at our farm. We advocate and follow a vegan raw food diet, but of course, volunteers can cook up anything vegetarian or vegan that they want. It is their choice. Well, this group decided that they would go raw for the two or three weeks that they spent with us. They had a talented 'cook' among them, and she was responsible for creating the meals. I am an award winning raw chef myself, but I have to admit that I learned a thing or two during their visit. One of them was fond of rock balancing, and left a rock sculpture at the entrance to our farm that still stands today.

Another time, we had a young lady who also decided that she would go raw during her stay with us. Unfortunately, sometimes the body is so toxic that when one attempts to go raw, it can make a person feel worse, before they feel better. This is because the raw food is very cleansing and it throws a lot of toxins into the blood stream. Still, when this young lady wasn't sleeping day and night, she tried to do some work. I remember that she planted a large bed of flower bulbs. I anxiously waited for them to emerge, but they never did. It turns out that she had planted them upside down. A few months after her visit, I heard from her and she thanked me for introducing her to the raw food diet. She said that she had continued on the diet after she got home and had lost a lot of excess weight.

One time a young volunteer was weeding around some hazelnut trees, fertilizing with rock dust and putting down mulch. I was walking by, and she said there were a lot of wasps around. I took a look and there, attached to one of the trees was a large hornet's nest. Whew!! Her eyes got big as saucers, because she hadn't noticed it at all and was working very close to it. I told her, forget that tree, we'll do it another time.

Sometimes we get people that are either down on their luck, or between jobs, or need some quiet time to plan their next move. They may not be so interested in growing organic food, but they seem happy to have a temporary place to stay, and to be out in Nature. Other times we get people who are really interested in learning how to grow food organically, and they choose to work more hours than requested. They have as a goal the desire to own their own farm one day. They ask a lot of questions, and we have lots of good conversations. For them I have a small library of books and DVDs available.

Yet other times we have people who come, and rather quickly decide they made a mistake. So then, we hear some very interesting, and sometimes hilarious, reasons why they have to leave immediately, such as, I just got a call from my roommate, and my apartment in the city is flooding with water; my grandfather's house just burned down; I have to see a doctor for my PMS; I think I have Lyme disease; my publisher needs to see me ASAP; my partner can't handle the business without me; I think I have to start small, I'm going to work in the Community garden;…Please take me to the train!!

All in all, as a small farm, we really appreciate the assistance, company, humor and good times that volunteers provide. We are sure that most of them get something positive out of the experience as well."

Scott and Andrea, from Bending Willow Farm on Vashon Island, Washington, have hosted about 15 to 20 woofers since May of 2011. They have a lot of first time Wwoofers, and or Wwoofers from the west coast, but also have had interns from British Columbia, Japan, Australia, the Czech Republic, France, Vietnam, Israel, and South Africa.

They describe the interaction with their Wwoofers beautifully. "Wwoofing have as enabled to share our lifestyle and philosophies with young people from around the world - what it means to live a sustainable lifestyle. As our Wwoofer journal will attest, our interns have thoroughly enjoyed their time with us as we have with them. We have to admit we learn as much as we have shared. Many are very smart, educated, and talented. Mostly in their early to mid-20s, a few that are 18, 19, and a few in their 30s. Generally, everyone has been respectful and courteous and interesting.

We enjoy hearing what this generation is thinking and doing as our own children are about the same age or approaching college. We have many community dinners where we cook and eat the food from the garden, and share stories, and experiences. We have learned about ourselves, too. That we know more than we thought about our growing in the northwest as we have been here for over 20 years. We are not experts, but we always have a large bounty of food by August. Our produce is for our own consumption, giving away, and trading. We have learned to understand what it means to live communally, sharing chores and all. Just about every time an intern has been here we have felt it has been a positive experience. And, we think that the interns leave enriched and in high spirits."

Another interesting observation Scott and Andrea made was that in their experience most of the interns seemed to be from middle to upper class families with many of their parents being professionals - doctors, lawyers, engineers, a principal, professors. So the surprising thing to them is that even though this is a work exchange program, they are not really getting the lower income class young adults.

`Vivian Smotherman of Eden's Cove Farm also wrote an entire essay on the Wwoof experience and I have included it here as he wrote it, because I can't see leaving any of it out or altering his words. So in Vivian's words:

"When I first heard about WWOOF it was on an episode of TOSH.0, and the creepy über-hippy pot head that was proclaiming that it was his way of getting girls did not impress me as the kind of person who would belong to any sort of group I wanted to be involved with. I'm not saying we're any different, only that in our dreams we imagine ourselves to be. The next time I heard about it was when a co-worker of my wife's mentioned that he'd been a Wwoofer in Utah (of all places). It still sounded strange, but he was an upstanding guy whom we really liked and he had nothing but great things to say about his experiences on the program. More than that there was a sense of loss in his voice when he talked about it, almost regret that he no longer shared in that simple but elegant lifestyle.

Our farm was growing and my wife and I both had demanding full time jobs; so after a little investigating and a lot of soul-searching we decided to give it a try. We signed up, created a profile and sat back with all fingers and toes crossed hoping we didn't end up with a psycho, or rather an endless chain of lazy lay 'bouts hiding from the responsibilities of the real world. That fear could not have been farther from the amazing truth behind the people that embark on this adventure

It didn't take long for our very first applicants to send us emails. We talked endlessly about screening and the proper questions to ask, but in the end it was easy enough. Our second applicant moved in just weeks after we placed our ad. At the time (unknown to us) she had been Wwoofing at another farm across town and it wasn't exactly going as she had hoped. So with an undaunted spirit she came by for a visit, toured the farm and got a glimpse of who we were and what we needed and she was on board. For our part she seemed grounded, motivated, intelligent and above all ready, willing, and able to handle the never-ending adventure that life at Eden's Cove delivers.

She stayed with us for about three months and we loved and cherished every minute of our time with her. Even now, nearly two years after she has come and gone we remain very close friends who chat online, on the phone and even in person when conditions and time permits. We loved her dearly and when that first experience was finished we couldn't wait for what would come next. Not surprisingly now, every one of our Wwoofers has gone away and left us with the same feelings of friendships that would last a life time.

It would be a bit wordy to explain or describe

all the wonderful people that have made our little guest house their home but each one has left a wonderful and permanent impression on our lives and on our farm. Internationally we've shared our home with people from France, Japan, China, Russia, the Netherlands, Columbia and our fantastic Germans. It would be incorrect to pick any as our favorites because we loved them all and each experience has been different, but the Germans came and spent six months with us (by far our longest experience) and let us share an amazing half year with their three year old daughter as she got to experience life and growing up a little on an American farm. Our domestic Wwoofers have been no less amazing; from the nomadic couples living life on the road to the students seeking adventure during breaks between semesters. It's always a treat.

One wonderful tradition we started early on was decorating the guest house. We've asked every resident to leave the place a little bit brighter than when they arrived. All our Wwoofers have vibrant and creative souls at heart, so the collection of pictures, sculptures, drawings, and other pieces that now decorate that little apartment would rival many of the best art museums. That's of course my opinion, but then I do go to a lot of art museums around the world.

At the end of the day Wwoofing is a give and take relationship between the farmer and the volunteers. In our experience the more we strive to give our Wwoofers, the more they work to return the hospitality. We offer a clean, cozy and private little cabin and lots of good conversation, great food, and a little exploratory 'touristing' around Austin, Texas in exchange for a few precious and valuable hours every day that have helped take our dream leaps and bounds closer to the reality we're looking for. We've gotten irrigation systems dug, fencing run, raised bed gardens planted and tended to, and most importantly; consistent, loving and reliable care for our animals. Past the basics we've experienced an exchange of culture and ideas that have enriched our lives and that of our children who've been lucky enough to share in the journey with us.

Joining the program and creating our listing has by far been the biggest factor in the amazing growth we've enjoyed at Eden's Cove farm. We recommend the program to farmers and friends alike and even have a few aspirations of finding a time in our future when maybe we can slip away to a foreign country and try this from the other side.

A final fun story; we know a gourmet butcher here in town whom we introduced our first Wwoofer to. He immediately recognized the program and wished us all well telling us that he too had been a Wwoofer at one point in the past. His experience on a 'farm' in Portugal consisted of taking care of a pot plant and two cucumber vines and he wouldn't trade those memories for anything on earth."

Mary Falk of Love Tree Farmstead in Wisconsin describes her experience over the past five years as being very positive with the Wwoofers that she and her husband have hosted. Here is a nice twist: "Our biggest complaint in the past has been that they won't quit working when we tell them to quit!" (Dave and I have also been fortunate enough to have had several Wwoofers who went above and beyond expectations.)

The typical Wwoofer here has been interested in the care and handling of livestock and cares about the environment and enjoys outdoor recreational activity. We have formed some very strong bonds with the majority of the Wwoofers and continue to correspond with them today. Some of the Wwoofers have come back for second round of visits and there are a few who plan on visiting with their families next summer. "

So if friends wonder why we do this, we have dozens and dozens of positive benefits to share and be grateful for. It also helps that we very much enjoy a household that is multicultural and /or multigenerational. It seems that the majority of farm hosts who wrote or spoke to me also enjoy this part of Wwoofing very much.

"The farmer has to be an optimist, or he wouldn't be able to farm."

Will Rogers

Chapter Seven

Wrinkles within the World of Wwoofing

If I have painted a sunny picture, it is because in the vast majority of cases the Wwoof experience is a wonderful exchange between farmers and the volunteers. Particularly if there has been good communication throughout and if everyone has the integrity to fulfill what they promise. We found this to be true from our personal perspective, and in contacting numerous farms within the USA network, and the Hawaii network, the responses indicate that the same is true by and large.

Along with that, a certain measure of luck and timing in having the right people turn up at any particular farm and the ingredients are there for success...almost always.

Because, no matter what, as to be expected

there are potholes in paradise. It would be disingenuous to state that it always works well and I believe it is necessary and fair to point out some of the pitfalls. Not to say we (i.e. our personal situation, and hosts in general) have lost faith in the program. Most hosts, even after being very frustrated when these situations arise, know that the benefits when it works well are so good, that it would be foolish to just abandon the program. On the other hand some have chosen to do just that.

What could go wrong you may wonder? After all, it is a fair exchange; there is a give and take on both sides. Farmers are sharing knowledge and food and lodging; volunteers are extending their helping hands and able bodies in hard work while they learn and absorb the practices of organic farming and sustainable living. Presumably, promises were made before hand and one would expect these to be honored.

Hosts shared incidents of minor issues that didn't stop the exchange from working, but perhaps caused more effort than they felt necessary. One woman said that when they hosted four or five helpers at time it became more of a party-great for the kids-but requiring her to spend too much time "herding" everyone and keep them on task. She also changed her policy to limit internet and be unplugged more often than not, because she felt the volunteers became non-communicative and "out of touch", not unlike experiences of professors these days. This is very understandable as part of the program is trying to foster genuine social interaction and relating one to one.

Unfortunately things don't always go according to plan. By far the overwhelming complaint that I learned of from the farm hosts who communicated with me is the issue of no shows, last moment cancellations, and abrupt departures, and all of these are intertwined. Personally, it is the one drawback that we experienced on our farm, and it seems to be the only negative issue according to the other farm hosts.

When it first occurs, you wonder if it could have been prevented, you think that it must be an anomaly, and that surely people wouldn't break their word so easily. Sad to say it has happened to many farm hosts on many occasions. For myself it is an issue of integrity, and it is disturbing in part because by its very nature sustainable living and organic principles attract those who love the earth and are concerned with environmental issues, and appreciate where healthy food comes from, and have respect for people, just to mention a few interconnected values.

So to have someone thoughtlessly leave you stranded comes as a shock. On the practical side, more often than not a farmer has made plans for projects that the helper[s] will be working on, has made arrangements for the lodging, has purchased enough food, and most likely has turned away one or several other possible volunteers who have requested an exchange only to be told the space has been filled.

To be fair occasionally someone can fill at the last moment. Ironically some of our best Wwoofers came accidentally after we had a cancellation. And if we can't find last minute replacements perhaps we at least can look at the bright side in that those individuals lacking integrity would not have been ideal volunteers, so perhaps we are better off. However, the fact remains-we can brush it off and say it doesn't matter, but it does matter that people break their word that easily.

Usually when this happens they let you know just a few days beforehand, or sometimes only the day before, or in the worst case, you are at the airport and no one arrives as they haven't bothered to tell you, adding valuable time lost from the farm needlessly.

Annie from Bright Hope Farm in Missouri still recommends the Wwoof experience to any one with the patience to teach what you want them to learn and if you need an extra hand in exchange. She knows now that sometimes it will be just a helping hand, perhaps without the learning you hope for, or the ability for them to work independently may never happen for some, so you may actually lose time supervising depending on a given task.

Mary Thompson of Kara Kahl Farm in Houston, Minnesota shared her reflections in the following essay.

Impressions of the Wwoofing program

by a Farm Host

We are finishing up our fourth year hosting Wwoofers and will definitely do it again next year. This program has really enriched our lives with the interesting people that it has brought to our door from all over the world.

The best part of the program is getting to

know these people and having them share their lives with us and to learn about their countries and cultures if they have come to us internationally. We enjoy visiting with them over meals or while doing work on the farm or perhaps going on 'field trips' in the area. We generally incorporate these folks into our family life (whatever is happening at the time) and they have the opportunity to participate in a wide variety of experiences ranging from showing dairy goats at fairs and shows, working at the yearly county garden tour, or long range errands (road trips) generally related to our farm. We also take them on picnics, boating on the Mississippi River, and try to allow some time for sightseeing in our area. Certainly it depends upon their interests and if they have their own transportation or not. If they choose to take time to follow their own interests in the area that works out too. We had a Wwoofer a couple years ago who had his own transportation and joined a local sailing group on the Mississippi River for the summer.

This year we are planning to visit two Wwoofers we have hosted from France when we go there later this year. We are having some Wwoofers return (more as friends) for repeat visits and we treasure these relationships. This year a young woman from Japan who spent the summer Wwoofing here will be coming back to spend the Christmas holidays with us before she returns home.

The second best thing about hosting Wwoofers is the work that they do here. Spring and summer are very, very busy with our large garden and also our herd of dairy goats. Their help is invaluable to us and we are able to accomplish so much more because of it. They bring a varied amount of expertise as well as have varied interests in what they want to learn. Some are very experienced in gardening and we've learned techniques and incorporated information they've shared with us into our gardening practices. Some really want to learn about dairy goat management and take advantage of all the opportunities to learn about them while here. Some of the international Wwoofers want to improve their English language speaking ability and are using the family stay as a way to speak English in every day conversation while not needing to worry about room and board.

We find that it works best to ask prospective Wwoofers about their expectations when we are first communicating in an effort to ensure that what we have to offer matches their goals. We can truly say we've never had a bad experience with a Wwoofer and would accept any that we've had back again.

That's not to say we haven't clicked better with some than others and that some are innately harder workers than others.

As far as frustrations the biggest is when a Wwoofer cancels out at the last minute. We understand how this can happen and will be consequently understanding about it but it is frustrating when we have turned other prospective Wwoofers away when we believe we are 'full'. We do always give feedback and ask that our Wwoofers provide feedback to us as we believe it gives the program more integrity and provides a mechanism for screening. We do not have a Wwoofer sign any type of contract or agreement. So far we've been very fortunate in having pretty good communication prior to agreeing for them to come and as stated earlier all our Wwoofers to date have been ones we've enjoyed having in our home and would welcome back.

Linda from McDonald Ranch had this to say in relation to the benefits and drawbacks of hosting: "We try to keep at least three guests (Wwoofers) here at a time. Since my husband and I work non-stop and because we are older, we find that having more than one guest at a time is essential not only because there is that much work to do on the farm, but also to provide a social support during their off time. We often have six to eight guests at once, but I must say that having so many tends to become a bit problematic because they tend to socialize so much that less and less work is done on the ranch yet our expenses of having the guests goes up. There are more lights, computers, and electric blankets left on costing more on the utility bill, much more wear and tear on the home and furnishings and, of course, more cost for food plus gas to transport them to places they want to go on their off time.

Even though we have house rules about cleaning up after oneself, there are always dishes to clean, floors to mop from muddy/dirty boots, bedding to wash, etc. So, at this point, I can't say that more resident volunteers have paid off with more work being done and, in fact, it seems to be a break-even at best. Still, we enjoy the company and exchange of information and the guests certainly enjoy their off-time social time on the ranch. "

Somewhat related to this issue are volunteers who seemingly are sincere and very interested in what you offer and knowing what to expect, and they agree to specific time commitments of anywhere from a week or two, to a month or more, but really they were more interested in the adventure and when they figure out how to travel on their own, or with another

Wwoofer they have met at your farm, they suddenly depart, and worse, often times with no explanation.

Farmers are left bewildered knowing only that these people said one thing and did another, that the communication wasn't really honest.

Michael Walkup of Walkup Farm and Heritage Gardens in Illinois has had his share of unfortunate experiences in regards to sudden cancellations after some volunteers were briefly working on the farm. In his case they were usually students, often from nearby Chicago, who committed to brief work stays during school breaks. Apparently each of them bailed when friends nearby called with more fun alternatives, particularly when they were ones who turned out ill-prepared for the hard work. He believes that has to stop accepting anyone under twenty-seven as they have each proven unreliable. Other hosts aim for no one under twenty-one or two as they find them less mature in general.

This is in marked contrast to what most farm hosts feel about young 20 somethings. Kelly from Mountain Edible Arts prefers those 20 somethings who want to get back to the earth, and love to learn and cook, and are motivated for both work and play. However, we each have different experiences and people to deal with, so it is hard to dismiss entirely.

Michael did appreciate that the Wwoofers who were a bit older were also more mature. However, he is dismayed with the work ethic he experienced and believes they will have a hard time when they enter the work force.

He still belongs to WWOOF and is building more accommodation, so he will not have to turn Wwoofers away for lack of room. This will alleviate the problem of being without any help if he finds himself with any more sudden departures.

One host shared that she accepts as many as they possibly have accommodation for, even if the number is higher than desirable, knowing full well that approximately 75% will be no shows. She realizes that they likely have sent requests to at least ten other farms and will not let the "unchosen" know their choice.

When hosts relayed similar stories the same theme repeats itself. Farmers depend on Wwoofer promises of being there for a given time period and plan their time around the promised availability, so it really causes problems when Wwoofers take it so cavalierly.

In most of these shared stories the Wwoofers weren't even unhappy with the work. Dissatisfaction or an inability to handle the work are issues that can also arise, and sometimes it is necessary for both parties to just agree it is not working out. It may still cause problems, but there is no mutual benefit if both sides aren't satisfied, so one must accept this.

However, it is the lack of respect and thoughtlessness that causes the true frustration. When hosts treat helpers like family and they leave with no explanation it is hard to believe.

We also had some of these disturbing situations. It happened once with two young French students who were eager to go camping on the weekend, and had stated they were planning to end their trip with a couple of weeks of pure travel around the island via camping. We went out of our way to take them to a great beach camping spot that was very affordable, only to have them tell us when we picked them up and brought them home Sunday evening for dinner that "they didn't need to Wwoof anymore since it was so easy and affordable to camp". Now they were taking the entire two months for vacation and they left in the morning, leaving us stranded and stunned, and disappointed that we were instrumental in helping them plan their getaway.

Another Austrian woman who had been on a

work exchange in Canada before coming here arrived on a Saturday morning and just loved our farm. She enjoyed it immensely all weekend, including all the great food. Monday morning she worked for three hours, and shocked us after lunch by telling us she had been experiencing personal problems the last week and had to leave immediately to return to Europe. Inexplicably, when we asked why she came to us , knowing she had these urgent problems, she admitted she just wanted to experience Hawaii and since she had already made plans to come here she did so she could at least be on a farm for a little while-knowing full well she would not stay. This one was so odd we had to dismiss it as pure craziness. We've had several others cancel before arriving-and ironically even as I write this book with all my genuine love of Woofers we are without helpers for this very reason.

We always stress in our communication how important the time commitments are as we plan accommodation accordingly. They always are aware of this, but some obviously don't care. Fortunately for us, even though we hate when this happens-in particular the lack of integrity-we are not dependent on Wwoofers per se because our crop of cacao is a couple of years away, and the rest of the fruit and vegetables are all for our use. It certainly slows us down- the weeds grow rapidly here- but we are not trying to get produce to a CSA or to a Farmers' Market, so we can work it out.

There are some farmers who tell the ones who are upset by these cancellations, and departures, and no-shows that they should not depend on the Wwoofers, but should consider them extra help that they are lucky to have if they show. Good advice in an ideal world. But not everyone can be, or is in this situation. And I see no reason not to expect integrity.

There are many hosts willing to take time to teach and to give away accommodation in trade that otherwise could be rented out, and to supply food they buy , or that they grow, that could be sold –for the desired trade in extra hands . It is a fair exchange and there is nothing wrong in expecting people to keep their word. Many hosts expressed that that is exactly how they run their farms and that-luckily-it works out well.

I read on an old forum, when we first encountered the problem that one host decided to rent out the accommodation instead of continuing with Wwoofing after it happened once too many times to him, and he now uses the income for paid helpers.

Even if hosts are not reliant on helpers the fact remains that it denies the opportunity for another Wwoofer who may be fully sincere in seeking a placement, so it does a disservice to their fellow peer groups as well as the hosts. One neighbor has implemented a system of requiring a deposit from helpers, which he refunds in full when they complete their service. Other hosts discussed this too, but usually concluded it would be negative and felt it would not attract the kind of helper they want.

But others remain aware of the way volunteers can and do use the host farm as a resting place while they figure out where to travel next. (And they may be using your computer and internet to plan their "escape".) Most often the ones who leave before completing the amount of time they said they would stay were just looking for a vacation.

Some of them do not distinguish between WWOOF, and Helpx, which is geared more for travelers who are willing to trade work for a place to stay, but are not here primarily, or even at all interested to learn about organic lifestyles and practices or sustainability. Worse still is if they assume it is no different than Couchsurfing and are looking for a free place to stay. Both of those organizations offer different services which are great-they are just very different than Wwoofing. We have however done exchanges with Helpxers that have worked out fine. We each knew beforehand what to expect of one another.

That seems to be the determining factor of whether the host will get and keep good helpers. Doing as much communicating before arrivals and during the stays will ensure a very high percentage of things going smoothly. Beyond that we have to accept that things can still go wrong and we may experience those dreaded cancellations and departures.

It is not generally a result of Wwoofers being mistreated or unhappy with the farm, according to many that expressed opinions on this matter. You can do everything right and just have that occasional dud that Eric mentioned.

Gene from the Last Word Ranch had this to say regarding the only real downside I could discern that he experienced from all he shared on Wwoof hosting. "By far we are too lenient and most of them wind up poring over our library and spending more time reading than working, eating my treats and eventually drinking my beer uninvited at which point we start easing them on down the road to some other experience where they can grow in a different way with someone else willing to give them a ride."

Mary and Dave of Love Tree Farm have had a very favorable Wwoof experience, yet Mary has these insights to share about the drawbacks they have also experienced.

"The typical Wwoofer here has been interested in the care and handling of livestock and cares about the environment and enjoys outdoor recreational activity. We have formed some very strong bonds with the majority of the Wwoofers and continue to correspond with them today. Some of them have come back for second round of visits and there are a few who plan on visiting with their families next summer. We have a simple questionnaire that we ask that they complete before we decide whether or not they will be a good fit here and usually the questionnaire acts as a good screening mechanism to catch folks that are perhaps "not quite such a good fit"...however, after this past summer it appears that I will need to revamp our questionnaire!

From what I have seen this past summer, there has been quite a few "desperados" on the road that have fudged their answers and once they are here it quickly becomes obvious that they aren't a good fit. This has been the only summer where we have repeatedly had 'issues' with the volunteers.

242

It appears that they don't want to really be here, rather they are looking for a place to 'hang out' while in between jobs, apartments, or they just don't want to be at home with mom and dad during the summer. Perhaps if we were vegetable gardeners it wouldn't be so obvious, but when working with livestock, a bad attitude can make not only for a long work day but can also put other people (besides themselves) in danger.

The common denominator is that the average age is between 20-24 and they are obsessed with texting, (so much so that I have had to ban the cell phones during chores and at the dinner table)...and...they have come from rather well to do suburbs. This is the only time that I have ever been 'made' to feel that I lead a sub-par life and I live in a hovel. This is the first summer where I ever had volunteers make repeated comments about having to work 'for free' or they were 'slave labor'. Some of them were visibly upset and it quickly became obvious that they were expecting more of a B& B 'farm stay' rather than be on a working farm....and only one of them liked animals!

There was also a real problem with initiative; if they weren't told to explicitly do something, it didn't get done, even if they had been told every day for a week to do the same chore, but I believe that goes hand in hand with simply not having the interest in really being here. All, (except one) were either college students or recent graduates. Interesting to note, the one who was not 'college' material got along just fine.

We also only had negative issues with the American volunteers, not the visiting Europeans or Chinese, but I attribute that difference to the fact that the international volunteers had made a substantial monetary investment in their visit and they were serious about learning what they could to make it worth their while...Sigh..."

Now they are focusing on the pleasant experiences of the past while they learn from the present. She is going to revamp their questionnaire and press harder for more info.

A couple of hosts noticed that as the job market improves the percentage of no shows has increased. Indeed some have had applicants tell them after accepting a Wwoof exchange that they now have accepted an "unexpected "job offer. Surely they knew they had applied for a job when they committed to come to a farm, but for some reason they feel justified in hedging their bets by accepting all offers and taking the best one for their situation in the end. I certainly was frustrated when this happened to us at the last minute.

Jim Long from Long Creek Herbs accurately describes one of the wrinkles we all encounter, namely in how some people do not become members, but instead borrow a friend's directory. It seems invariably if this is true, then the result is someone who is only marginally interested, and will most likely not be a benefit to your farm; this reminds us all of how important it is to check profiles.

Another category of Wwoofers he has been in contact with (and we have seen this as many hosts have,) are the ones who attempt to come at the last moment. Jim has actually had a Wwoofer show up without prior inquiry; he believes in being polite and that connecting in advance is just a common courtesy. It is an indication of a possible problem if arrangements have not been made beforehand.

"For example, if one does let a last minute arrival stay, how likely is that person to follow other simple rules on your farm"? Jim pointed out..

That situation brings to mind the ones who don't read the listings or respond in any way to your listing, but just send generic emails. To many of us it indicates a prospect that doesn't have a genuine interest in learning, or in farming if so little effort is made in communicating. These are Wwoofers who get weeded out beforehand. One of the worst I have received is this brief sentence:

"hey, i would like to come work on your farm whenever you have an opening next. let me know when that will be. thanx, xxxxx

I never cease to be amazed at these types of requests since they clearly have not read the listing (e.g. we always indicate when openings are available) offer no information as to why we might have a (good) exchange, nor state anything about themselves whatsoever. I wish these would-be helpers well, but they must start with reading the WWOOF USA and WWOOF HAWAII web sites when they become members to have a basic understanding of the process they hope to become part of one day.

Jim's last example is not one that has occurred with us as we farm year round in our climate, but I know that is simply not the case for most seasonal farms, so other hosts may have similar cases.

Each year he has a couple of applicants who

want to come to the farm around February, just before spring break, and it has also happened in January too, in the dead of winter. Being in Missouri there is nothing happening on his farm during those months. He again feels this indicates no sincere interest in farming, if they have not learned about the seasons and gardening. Along with this lack of basic knowledge, he found his own inquiries about their interests in coming to the farm to be overly vague-to the point of being secretive about themselves, so he chose to follow his instinct and not offer an opening. (Amusingly, he named it the 'moonglow and cloud syndrome' as in his experience he gets some similar applicants every year and he found coincidentally that these applicants tended to have obscure, unusual names such as these.

Rhio, from Rhio's Gardens, added a few of her less than optimal experiences.

"We have had two negative experiences. The following is one of them. A couple came to our place because an adjacent town was evicting them from a resort where they had been working. The resort was being cited and closed down for some building violations. All the people staying there were evicted. So, the couple came to our place as volunteers, and they brought a camper, which they parked on our property, and stayed in. At first everything was fine (couple of months). Then they had some domestic problems, and the young lady left. After that the young man became different. He still did some work, but hardly. Then, he left for an extended time (a few months), and left all his stuff and his camper. When he returned, he reneged on doing the five hours of work we ask for each day, six days a week. He became argumentative and even said that we should pay him as caretaker. By this time, it was winter, and it was too cold to stay in the camper, so, out of concern and kindness, we invited him into the house.

Later, we found out that he had been taking some street drugs, and that is probably what caused his changed attitude and behavior. The funny thing about it is that he was instrumental in getting his girlfriend off of drugs, only to fall victim to them himself.

This experience led us to plan on building a separate residence for ourselves as soon as we are able.

She ends on this note, a view many hosts shared: "We try not to let the negatives color our view of what new people could bring into our experience. All in all, as a small farm, we really appreciate the assistance, company, humor and good times that volunteers provide. We are sure that most of them get something good out of the experience as well".

Finally, in all of my research I came across just one farmer who was rather disenchanted with the program. Jim Milner operates a successful olive grove, Le Ferme Soleil, (aka The Sunny Olive Farm) in Winters, California. The farm produces purely organic olive oil that is sold commercially. He has had several Wwoofers, but felt it was actually too expensive for him to continue as they cost him too much in time and broken equipment. Since his was only one of two actual negative letters I had received, I inquired if he had anything positive to say about the experience, but unfortunately he could only say that while he wanted to be more positive that was his experience.

In his words: "I think WWOOF is brilliant in concept, but needs wider appeal to get the job done." His conclusions included suggesting better screening beforehand, checking up on references, having a zero tolerance rule regarding alcohol and drugs, and aiming to get Wwoofers to sign an agreement for the length of their commitment.

The other strictly negative email only indicated that the host had dealt with dishonest helpers who allegedly stole things during their stay and when they left after being less than helpful while there, and were "running from the law". She felt the only good helpers she had had over five years hosting were middle-aged and that they were far and few between. I have nothing else of this nature in my voluminous correspondence.

No one has offered a sure fire way to weed out or eliminate the insincere or vagabond Wwoofer who never intended to keep a commitment in the first place. After the fact, we can add comments to their profiles, or use the forums, and in this way forewarn other hosts. And I have had hosts write me and say that they prevented possible problems by reading about advice given by hosts on the forums regarding specific persons to avoid. But mostly we first just have to use our own judgment, read between the lines a bit, try to read the warning signals when they change in mid-stream, and hope for the best.

Alina Joy Du Bois from The Good Old Days Farm in Texas is a fairly new host. She has only hosted a very few Wwoofers so far-not for lack of trying- as she is very enthusiastic; these Wwoofers weren't able to stay long initially, but are making plans to return soon, much to her delight, as she found all of them to be fantastic helpers.

Again and again most hosts say the benefits far outweigh the negatives, so of course we move on and look forward to the next joyful encounter.

For those of you who are new to organic agriculture and /or sustainable living who are considering hosting Wwoofers, I recommend giving it a try, taking some of the advice shared from the hosts, and having your own Wwoofing adventure. You won't really know what it is like until you try it, regardless of what you are told or read. Each experience will be unique and more than likely be a positive and beneficial exchange for all involved-one more seed planted to grow the organic movement.

"The only way to build hope is through the Earth."

Vandana Shiva

Chapter Eight

Closing Conversation: The Future for Organic Farming, Sustainable Living, and Wwoofing

At this point in time, Organic Farming only represents a small percentage of the farming and food production in our country and worldwide, despite the huge increases in consumer demand and awareness, but the horizon appears very promising.

Ironically all food was grown organically until people came along with perhaps the best of intentions and implemented their labor saving methods with industrialized agriculture. Abandoning small farm farming methods has drastically changed the soil as well as food production. Arguments abound currently with some scientists still attempting to convince us organically produced food is no better for us nutritionally.

Most people reading this will be proponents of organic food and strongly disagree as we seek more nutritious, pesticide free food. One of the leading activists in this field, Dr. Vandana Shiva is very outspoken with her views regarding how misleading this information can be. She works tirelessly to promote biodiversity and conservation and for farmers' rights through her *Research Foundation for Science, Technology, and Ecology.* She states the case for organic sustainable farming that feeds the world without harming the planet's resources or the health of the population in numerous publications worldwide, arguing against what she perceives as myths regarding industrialized ag's ability to produce more food.

For example, despite the collective ability of the world's population to produce enough food to feed everyone on the planet, we still have nearly a billion people in the world who do not get sufficient food and are therefore hungry; correspondingly approximately one billion people are suffering from malnutrition. Particularly in developed countries with mass quantities of food available to us, more and more people get by on cheap, over-processed, low nutrient food.

The realities are that industrialized agriculture

relies heavily on chemicals and fossil fuels at the expense of reducing labor needs. It has created an inefficient and wasteful system of producing food, for example, with grain fed factory farms versus the grass fed free range ecosystems described on many of the Wwoof farms.

The chemicals have depleted the soil so much that necessary mineral nutrients are missing from modern food. And our health depends on good food and therefore on the soil in which it is grown.

There are no easy or quick solutions to these problems. The food revolution exists however, and the organic movement and Wwoof continue to help us get to the next stages of better food production worldwide.

In fact globally, mostly in developing and underdeveloped countries of course, despite the industrialization of agriculture, small farms still produce most of the food in the world. Most of that food is consumed regionally or 'locally' as we call it. Another irony is that perhaps they are still getting more nutritious food since they can't afford the chemical intensive methods of industrial agriculture.

However, the fact remains that changes must be made in order to feed the world. At (MIT)

Massachusetts Institute of Technology a student-managed class called Terrrascope has proposed their current project as *Mission 2014: Feeding the World,* and they are seriously examining the problems of food shortages and how to provide nutritious food globally.

Some of their conclusions are that inevitably we cannot expect to just switch over to organic methods worldwide overnight and achieve good results. As any of us already growing food with organic methods realizes, it takes time to grow good food, it takes time to improve the soil, and it takes much labor-as the Wwoofers will attest to.

And while there are higher labor demands and higher costs with somewhat lower yields (while of course higher yields are possible with methods such as Natural Korean Farming and Biodynamics to name a few), strictly using organic methods cannot be expected on a wide-scale basis –at least not yet.

But a progressive solution seems quite realistic where with time it can be achieved. There needs to be a compromise initially between industrial methods and organic sustainable ones creating a gradual permanent shift back to healthy farming and thereby producing sufficient quantities of food that are also dense with nutrients and absent of harmful pesticides.

One of the tougher challenges is the modern marriage of industrialized agriculture with (GMOs) genetically modified organisms where the giant corporate proponents tell us that by integrating these two elements they can create more disease resistant crops and higher yields still.

But this again takes us into the realms of more unknown dangerous chemicals and the larger unknowns of the long-term effects on us. This is a huge topic, once again outside the scope or intention of this book, but a subject that all of us who believe in the organic movement come up against.

Ultimately, while there may need to be a compromise globally as there is no easy fix for the world food production, we do have the power and ability to be in control of what we eat here and now. We will continue to grow food via sustainable cyclic methods which are so simple and real and have and had worked for centuries. We can raise livestock who produce both food for us and manure to feed the vegetable crops which in turn provides more nutritious food for our families and for the livestock, thereby continuing the cycle.

One more interesting aspect I came across

through my research is the apparent success of organic farming growing into larger farms, without sacrificing these good sustainable farming methods as they grow.

The best example I found was for *Stonyfield Organic* producing organic yogurt. Gary Hirshberg was the co-founder, and is the author of <u>Stirring It Up: How to Make Money and Save the World</u>, and co-author of <u>Label It Now: What You Need to Know About Genetically Engineered Foods</u>. He frequently speaks on the topics of sustainability, the profitability of green business and organic agriculture, among other topics and is an advocate for change in national food and agriculture policies, including those regarding the labeling of genetically engineered foods.

I found it fascinating to learn that their farm business grew from a seven-cow organic farm,(which he began after he was a teacher at a small rural farming school), into a company with $360 million in annual sales.

I don't believe the intention of small organic farms in the USA who are partnering with volunteer Wwoofers have ambitions of becoming such large-scale farms, but I mention it here because as the demand for organic food increases we may not be able to provide for all the demand beyond supplying

Farmers' Markets, CSAs and local shops and restaurants. Therefore, other farms on a larger scale may be necessary as part of the organic movement, and I think it is good that people are doing this who are also dedicated to preserving the ideals and principles of organic, sustainable farming as they grow.

Another point is that not all farms are able to work on all levels necessary for the complete sustainable cycles described earlier, but most are striving to get there. Once again we are reminded that it takes time to change over soil that was depleted before any of us started farming and much labor to keep things growing and weeded and mulched and pruned, and to feed animals and provide their food-all to keep that cycle going. But the good news is that it is all doable and the farms described within these pages are doing it now.

With the continued exchanges between Wwoof hosts and Wwoofers the organic movement will continue to grow and we can all be satisfied with the happiness of eating great food grown by ourselves and additionally in providing it for those who are not able to grow it but are willing and able to buy it via those Farmers' Markets and CSAs and local restaurants and shops.

The executive director of WWOOF USA, Sarah Potenza, offered her thoughts on the future with these comments which I think is a fitting closure for this book:

"At WWOOF-USA, we are very excited about the future of WWOOF and building its connection to the organic movement. We are incredibly grateful to our wonderful hosts and members who joined WWOOF over the past ten years of WWOOF-USA's operation.

Every day, our members help to create a reality of our mission: to be part of a worldwide effort to link visitors with organic farmers, promote an educational exchange, and build a global community conscious of ecological farming practices. Wwoofer membership has doubled in recent years, and host numbers continue to steadily increase. More and more people are making connections through WWOOF and learning to share and grow the organic lifestyle.

We are inspired daily by their efforts and enthusiasm for Wwoofing. And this phenomenon is not happening just in the USA. WWOOF is a global movement, now found in more than fifty countries worldwide, with new WWOOF groups starting each year from all corners of the planet: Serbia to Burundi to Venezuela, and beyond. WWOOF is found on every continent (except Antarctica!). There is an incredible momentum to grow WWOOF in support of a worldwide effort to help farmers provide nutritional food while growing the organic movement through an educational exchange.

We think these are amazing times to be a part of WWOOF in any country, and we are thrilled to see where Wwoofing in the USA leads us in the future.

Happy Wwoofing everyone!"

APPENDIX

Directory of Contributing

WWOOF Host Farms

—————————————————————

7B Ranch	Petrolia, California
20 Mile Farm	Two Rivers, Alaska
A New Earth Farm	Harlingen, Texas
Ajila Ama Farm	Brasstown, North Carolina
Alaska's Ridgewood Wilderness Lodge	Homer, Alaska
Angelheath	Raton, New Mexico
Anima Botanical Wildlife Sanctuary	Reserve, New Mexico
Apple Pond Farm	Callicoon Center, New York
Bending Willow Farm	Vashon Island, Washington
Biotechture Training	Bullard, Texas

Birds & Bees Community Farm	*Oregon City, Oregon*
Blueberries Galore	*Saginaw, Michigan*
Blue Heron Farm	*Pittsboro, North Carolina*
Bobcat Ridge Avocados	*Watsonville, California*
Borner Farm Project	*Prescott, Wisconsin*
Branch Out Farm	*Soquel, California*
Branched Oak Farm	*Raymond, Nebraska*
Bright Hope Farm	*Hughesville, Missouri*
Bug Hill Farm	*Ashfield, Massachusetts*
Casa Rosa Farms	*Madera, California*
Case Country Road Farm	*Glade Spring, Virginia*
Catskill Mt Natural Agriculture	*Hunter Valley, New York*
Classic Organic Farm & Market	*Gaviota, California*
Claymont Community	*Charles Town, West Virginia*
CloudPlay Homestead	*Gold Beach, Oregon*
Cold Creek Ranch	*Clifton, Arizona*
Comfort Eagle Bamboo Farm	*La Belle, Florida*
Country Gardens Farm	*Yale, Oklahoma*
Cross Island Farms	*Wellesley Island, New York*
Desert Land	*Tucson, Arizona*
Doubletree Farm	*Marshall, North Carolina*
EagleSong Family Peony Farm	*Wasilla, Alaska*

Earthkeeper Farm	Kent City, Michigan
Earthly Elements Farm	Madelia, Minnesota
Elk Creek Gardens	Trail, Oregon
Energy Farm	Oakland, Nebraska
Eden's Cove	Cedar Creek, Texas
Fable Farm	Barnard, Vermont
FalsterFarm & Cattle Ranch	Winnsboro, Texas
Farm on Kitchen Branch	Greeneville, Tennessee
Fennario Farm	Barrington, Rhode Island
Fieldsong Farm	Manutuck, Rhode Island
Finca Pedro Gordo	Florida, Puerto Rico
Finney Farm	Concrete, Washington
Flower to Flour	Mt. Hood, Oregon
Forever Yong Farm	Amado, Arizona
For the Love of Bees	Dixon, New Mexico
Fresh Apple Cider Orchards	Paonia, Colorado
Foundation Farm	Eureka Springs, Arkansas
Geyser Farm	Livingston, Montana
Goodness Grows	Bedford, Pennsylvania
Greendale Farm	Madison, Georgia
Greenleaf Farm	Makawao, Hawaii
Green Fire Farm & Winery	Hoopa, California
Green String Farm	Petaluma, California

Happy Hydroponics	Pukwana, South Dakota
Hard Cider Homestead	Ringoes, New Jersey
Harmony Hill	Exeter, California
Heartland Farm	Pawnee Rock, Kansas
Hell's Backbone	Boulder, Utah
Hot Springz	Mecca, California
Howling Husky Homestead	Homer, Alaska
Irish Ridge Ranch	Half Moon Bay, California
Island Goode's	Hilo, Hawaii
JCK Family Farm	Scottsville, Kentucky
Joe's Nuts	Captain Cook, Hawaii
Ka Ulu O Kalani	Kealakekua, Hawaii
Kalapana Organics	Kalapana, Hawaii
Kara Kahl Farm	Houston, Minnesota
La'akea Community	Pahoa, Hawaii
La Ferme Soleil [AKA The Sunny Olive]	Winters, California
Last Word Ranch	Cerrillos, New Mexico
Le Vin Organic Winery & Vineyards	Cloverdale, California
Long Creek Herbs	Blue Eye, Missouri
LoveTree Farmstead	Grantsburg, Wisconsin
Laurel Valley Creamery	Gallipolis, Ohio
Maggie's Herbs	St. Augustine, Florida
Maravilla Mountain	Las Marias, Puerto Rico

McDonald Ranch	Santa Rosa, California
Merlin's Perch	Carmel, California
Moonrise Farms	Concho, Arizona
Morningside Farm	Hinckley, Ohio
Mountain Edible Arts	Burnsville, North Carolina
MPG Ranch	Florence, Montana
MS Fit Ranch	Liberty, Missouri
Native Ideals Seed Farm	Arlee, Montana
New Earth Organic Farm	Colebrook, New Hampshire
North Creek Community Farm	Prairie Farm, Wisconsin
Olde Oak Farm	Maxfield, Maine
Pholia Farm	Rogue River, Oregon
Piedmont Herbs[at Blue Heron]	Pittsboro, North Carolina
Prairie Rose Organic Farm	Willow City, North Dakota
Prariana Farms	Clearmont, Wyoming
Quail Hollow Farm	Overton, Nevada
RainForestGlenn Farm	Papaikou, Hawaii
Red Fern Farm	Gray Court, South Carolina
Red House Farm	Boulder, Utah
Reevis Mountain School	Roosevelt, Arizona
Rhio's Garden	Eldred, New York
Rusty Plough Farm	Ellenville, New York
Sambo Berries	Pepeekeo, Hawaii

San Diego's Bucolic Farm	Rainbow, California
Sassafras Valley Farm	Morrison, Missouri
Second Chances	Mena, Arkansas
Shekinah Farm	Hazel Green, Alabama
Shepherds Green	Cookeville, Tennessee
Silver Wheel Farm	Harrisville, Pennsylvania
Spencer Creek Range	Eugene, Oregon
Springtree Community	Scottsville, Virginia
Stillpoint Lodge	Halibut Cove, Alaska
Stoneybrook Organic Farm	Hillsboro, Virginia
Sun One Organic Farm	Bethlehem, Connecticut
Supernatural Organic Farms	Ponchatoula, Louisiana
Sweet Breeze Farm	Onomea, Hawaii
Sweetwater Farm	Petersham, Massachusetts
Taos Goji	Cristobal, New Mexico
The Banana Patch	Kealakekua, Hawaii
The Good Farm	Berlin, Maryland
The Good Old Days Farm	Blue Ridge, Texas
The Poor Farm	Gentryville, Indiana
The Prairie Flower	Spencer, Iowa
The Small Family Farm	Sandpoint, Idaho
The Stone Fox Farm Creamery	Monroe, Maine
The Thankful Goat Farm	Granite Falls, North Carolina

Troutlily Farm	Hot Springs, North Carolina
Twin Brooks Farm	Chehalis, Washington
Udder View Farm	Columbia, Maine
Urbiculture Community Farms	Denver, Colorado
Walking Bear Ranch	Whitefish, Montana
Walking J Farm	Amado, Arizona
Walkup Heritage Farm & Gardens	Crystal Lake, Illinois
We Are All Farmers	Union Grove, North Carolina
We'Moon Land	Estacada, Oregon
Wild Wines	Jacksonville, Oregon
Wilder Thymes	Wilder, Minnesota
Wishful Acres	Lena, Illinois

ABOUT THE AUTHOR

Camille Glenn is a former ESL professor who has enjoyed traveling extensively around the globe--- and she still does. After living in a variety of places, she and her husband Dave have chosen to plant roots in Hawaii where they are growing cacao for future artisan chocolate with the help of WWOOFERS. She also enjoys creating art through painting and photography.

Made in the USA
San Bernardino, CA
06 December 2019